WANDERLUST

A Spiritual Travelogue
for the Adventurous Soul

WONDERLUST

A Spiritual Travelogue
for the Adventurous Soul

Vicki Kuyper

NEW HOPE
PUBLISHERS
Birmingham, Alabama

New Hope® Publishers
P. O. Box 12065
Birmingham, Alabama 35202-2065
www.newhopepublishers.com
New Hope® Publishers is a division of WMU®.

Library of Congress Cataloging-in-Publication Data
Kuyper, Vicki J.
Wonderlust : a spiritual travelogue for the adventurous soul / Vicki Kuyper.
      p. cm.
ISBN 978-1-59669-076-9 (sc)
1. Christian pilgrims and pilgrimages. 2. Christian life—Textbooks.
I. Title.
BV5067.K89 2007
263'.041—dc22
                            2007009948

Interior page photos for chapters 1, 2, 5, 6, 7, 9, 11, 12, 15, 17, 18, 19, 20, 21, 22, 26, 27, 28, and 29, courtesy of Cindy Miller Hopkins.

ISBN-10: 1-59669-076-3
ISBN-13: 978-1-59669-076-9
N074137 • 0907 • 15M1

To the Author of all my journeys

with heartfelt thanks for every traveling companion

He's brought my way.

Contents

Acknowledgments

Writing a book is a journey all its own—and I've shared this memorable journey with a host of adventurous souls. Heartfelt thanks goes to my "first readers," great lovers of books and of God: Pam Clark, Karen Pfander, Cynthia Helblig, Rita Puckett, and Brooke Boon. Your constructive criticism helped craft every chapter, while your giddy enthusiasm kept my spirits up whenever my confidence threatened to take a nosedive.

Gratitude also goes to my Thursday afternoon Bible study group. You've challenged and supported me in more ways than you know. The thought of each and every one of you brings a smile to my face and a prayer to my lips—along with an insatiable craving for coconut cupcakes.

I'm also deeply in the debt of my newfound travel companions at New Hope. If publishing houses were measured by the size of their heart, you'd be the biggest of them all. Andrea, Joyce, Tina, and Kathryne, you truly are an author's "dream team." There are not enough synonyms for "thank you" to fully express my appreciation for all you've done and continue to do.

As for my family, I'd be remiss if I didn't thank you for allowing me to share so much of our lives, warts and all, with total strangers. Cindy, not all sisters wind up as best friends. I'm so thankful we can be counted among the lucky ones. Ryan and Katrina, for the last two decades you've opened my eyes to wonder I would have passed right by if you weren't by my side. I'm so blessed God chose me to be your mom. And Mark, you are my knight in shining armor, even when you're wearing a T-shirt and gym shorts. I never imagined I could love anyone so deeply and that marriage could be this much fun! All my love, all my life . . .

Last, but by no means least, eternal thanks to my dear Abba Father. You know my heart. You know where I've come from and where I'm headed. I pray every journey I take leads me closer to You.

Our Itinerary

I first fell head over heels in love with the world's wonders in a library bookmobile. Once a week, I'd stand before the dented aluminum door of a musty mobile home as if I were Aladdin before the secret cave of Ali Baba, awaiting hidden riches to be revealed. It wasn't a magic phrase, but a library card that became my passport to adventure.

Although I was only 8 or 9 at the time, I found myself at home in the archaeology section. Here I stole my first glimpse of the tragedy of Pompeii, the mystery of Easter Island, and the majesty of Machu Picchu. Who needed fairy-tale castles and enchanted forests when there were magical places such as these that already existed in the world?

It wasn't until I turned 16 that my journeys advanced beyond the printed page. A willing stowaway on my father's business trip, I had the opportunity to explore the ancient treasures of Egypt, wander the markets of Casablanca, climb Paris's Eiffel Tower, and witness a solar eclipse off the deck of a cruise ship as we shadowed the coast of Africa. Never before had I experienced the awe and excitement that filled virtually every waking moment of those three weeks.

I didn't realize at the time that what was calling out so loudly to my soul was not simply a lust for travel, but a hunger for God, a longing to know the One who is the true Artist and Architect behind the real wonders of the world. I recognized His voice for the first time two years later—on yet another journey.

At a Christian camp located along the forested waterways of Canada I discovered what my heart was searching for. There, as I waterskied among whales and took quiet walks along pine needle-covered paths, I also took time to read the Bible for the very first time. I discovered that God is not a myth. He is as real as the ruins of Troy and the Great Wall of China. And this almighty God desires to have a relationship with me.

Out of all the journeys I've taken, it is this one—the one that leads me closer to God and toward becoming who He created me to be—that holds the most adventure, beauty, and unbridled joy. And it is on this journey that I invite you to become my traveling companion.

This inward journey can often be sparked by an outward journey. Whether you are already an avid traveler, or prefer to explore the world from the comfort of your easy chair, this book will take you around the globe. From hiking the Inca Trail to riding an elephant through the teak forests of Thailand to the wonders found in my own backyard, come with me to explore uncharted territories of the heart, both God's and your own.

> *Blessed are those whose strength is in you, who*
> *have set their hearts on pilgrimage.*
> Psalm 84:5 (NIV)

Journey Toward . . .
SELF-ACCEPTANCE

The Inca Trail,

Peru

*I*s it my imagination or are my hiking boots actually mocking me? With each rhythmic step on the rocky trail, they seemed to whisper, "Impostor, fraud, fool . . . What are you doing here?" Whether it was my imagination, the lack of oxygen at this altitude, or an actual protest staged by my brand-spanking-new purple footwear, one thing was certain. I totally agreed with my shoes.

New boots on a walk of 5 miles announce, "Amateur." On a four-day, 23-mile hike up the

Leaning against a rocky ledge for support, I frantically surveyed the summit once more. Maybe no one had noticed.

Inca Trail of Peru, they broadcast, "Accident waiting to happen." And from the way my head was spinning, my lungs were burning, and my recent breakfast was now tumbling like an Olympic gymnast in my stomach, it looked as though that accident would take place any moment. It seemed Warmiwanusca, which means "Dead Woman's Pass," was about to live up to her name.

I took my eyes off my boots for a moment to survey the formidable Dead Woman ahead. The trail looked like a chiseled scar, cutting its way up the face of the mountain to its 13,776-foot summit. No switchbacks for the Incas. They traveled the most direct route, despite the fact that there was half the oxygen at this altitude than there was at sea level.

Being from Colorado, I thought I knew all about functioning at high altitude. After all, I lived more than a mile above sea level. I could take the stairs in my home two at a time, unlike most of our out-of-town guests who found themselves winded just getting in the front door. I was certainly no flatlander. I even had to use high altitude directions when baking a cake. I figured that my 2-mile saunter each morning on the foothills near Pikes Peak in Colorado Springs would be adequate training to cover a mere 23 miles spread out over four days. However, my lungs, which felt as though they'd shrunk to the size of garbanzo beans, were now chiming in with my boots. "Unprepared . . . Out of breath . . . Out of shape . . . Who do you think you are?" they wheezed.

At that moment, who I was seemed undeniably clear. I was an almost 40-year-old mother of two. I had high blood pressure and was, apparently, aerobically challenged. I was the runt of the litter compared to my traveling companions: a girlfriend, who could be a poster child for the benefits of a gym membership; a tour company owner, who traveled all over the world and spoke several languages; our guide and his wife, who traveled this route several times every month; and our porters, who literally sprinted over the rocky trails wearing only tattered sandals on their feet and carrying their body weight in provisions on their backs.

I was the straggler, the tagalong, the misfit, falling into last place a mere five minutes after our journey began. In those first few moments, the porters had taken off down the trail like a pack of racehorses responding to the starting bell, their rainbow-colored ponchos flapping in the wind like jockey's silks. The rest of the group had fallen into a brisk pace behind them, chatting together easily as they made their way around the first corner of the trail—and out of my sight. I was left alone with my thoughts, and my bright purple boots, as the first raindrops began to fall. Soon, my tears became indistinguishable from the rain on my cheeks.

What am I doing here, God? I asked the only companion Who chose to remain by my side. Ever so gently, God rewound the tapes of my life, taking me back to my childhood and the archaeology book where I had first caught a glimpse of Machu Picchu. The ancient foundations of this fairy-tale fortress clung to a verdant mountain peak like stone fingers, hanging on for dear life. Its crumbling buildings promised to hold stories and secrets about a people who lived there 500 years ago. A people who had disappeared into thin air. A people who had done exactly what I'd wanted to do so often as a painfully shy little girl.

Machu Picchu promised to be the safe house a frightened child longed for. A place of peace and refuge, wonder and longing. A place where no one could find her, except maybe God Himself.

It was that little girl who beckoned me here. The one who wanted to climb the Inca Trail as if she were an explorer, instead of taking the train as a "tourist." The one who wanted to run her fingers along those ancient walls, to see with her own eyes the impossibly green cliffs and mysteriously shadowed valleys. *Where is that fit, energetic little 9-year-old girl when you need her?* I asked my plodding middle-aged self. I heard God whisper to my heart in reply. *She's right here with you. She's the one who wanted purple shoes. . . .*

Not wanting to disappoint the little girl within, I took another shaky step forward. As I glanced longingly up at the crest of the mountain, which was mottled with low-lying patches of mist, I saw that my traveling companions had already reached their morning destination. They were relaxing on the saddle of the summit, resting against their day packs, and enjoying the view—which included me about a quarter of a mile below them making my way up the trail with the speed of a proverbial sea slug. A sudden wave of altitude sickness brought my sluggish steps to a complete halt. Panicked, I recalled what our guide, Manolo, had said the evening before we began our trek. He'd explained that anyone who got sick would have to return to a lower altitude . . . go back to the hotel . . . be forced to abandon the trek. And although Manolo never said the words aloud, my mind added, *Would be a disgrace . . . an embarrassment . . . a burden to the rest of the group.*

I should have spoken up the night before. Even though our camp was perched only halfway up the Dead Woman's back, my body had already begun its revolt. But I couldn't give up. Not after I'd come so far. Instead of going to Manolo for help, I decided to keep my condition under wraps. As a precaution, I took enough Imodium to dam the Amazon. Unfortunately, there are other routes by which an errant breakfast can escape. And escape it did.

Leaning against a rocky ledge for support, I frantically surveyed the summit once more. Maybe no one had noticed. Maybe I could pull myself together enough to keep moving forward. Maybe I could go on pretending I was "just fine."

But Manolo was already sprinting down the path toward me, followed by a poncho-clad porter carrying a first-aid kit and an oxygen tank. The sight of them retracing all of the hard-earned steps they had just completed on the way up made my heart sink even lower. At that moment, I wholeheartedly remembered how I had felt as a child. Small. Weak. Dependent. And all I wanted to do was disappear. But that was not an option.

In a matter of minutes, I felt Manolo's hand rest on my trembling shoulder. His voice was gentle and compassionate, like someone trying to coax a frightened bird out of the corner of a cage. I gathered the courage to lift my head and look into his eyes. What I saw was kindness and concern. Not a hint of condemnation. Not a trace of annoyance. Not a word about turning back. With the bedside manner of a loving parent, he assessed my physical condition and then did something unexpected. He sent the porter and the medical supplies back up the mountain.

As the porter's footsteps, quick and surefooted as ever, grew more distant, Manolo turned to look me straight in the eye. "Do you know why you are always last?" he asked gently. "It's because you are looking at the mountains. You are studying the wildflowers. You are taking pictures. You are on a journey. And the others? They are concerned about being first. They hurry. They compete. They want to be the first one to the camp. At the end of this trip, who will hold the most beautiful memories?"

I glanced back down at my boots, as embarrassment overtook me once more. But this time, it was not born out of my weakness or perceived inadequacies. I was embarrassed at having been *seen*, for being visible—and for someone having liked what he saw.

Manolo continued, "For the last two days, you've been working so hard to keep up with everyone else. You've pushed yourself to walk at their pace instead of your own. But each of us was created with our own pace. You need to be true to yours, not theirs.

"Right now, you need to learn the 'walk of the patient one.' It isn't called this because others have to be patient with *you*. It's because you have to learn to be patient with *yourself*. You put one foot just one inch in front of the other. Then you do the same with the other foot. Little by little you'll make your way up the mountain. I know it will feel slow. But if you move forward like this, you'll regain your strength and you won't have to stop and rest along the way.

"I'll give you a choice," Manolo said. "We can either walk together up the mountain in silence, practicing the 'walk of the patient one,' or as we walk I can tell you stories about the people who once walked these mountains." One choice he did not offer was giving up.

The stories of the Incas called to me as vividly as they had back in that bookmobile so many years ago. So I put one foot one inch in front of the other as I listened to Manolo's voice, his English rising and falling like a condor riding the air currents of his native Peruvian tongue. . . .

"Messengers used to run, not walk, this Royal Road. That's what the Incas called the trail we're on now. For 15,000 miles, from modern-day Ecuador to the coast of Chile, this network of footpaths wound its way through dense jungles and over mountain peaks up to 20,000 feet high. Manned relay posts were spaced several miles apart, so messengers working in tandem could cover up to 250 miles a day. Back then it took less time to deliver a message from one end of the Inca empire to the other than it often does for a letter to travel across Peru today.

"The Royal Road itself was beautiful, covered with smooth white stones and framed by a border of wildflowers. Carrying messages or fresh fish for the Incan emperor, the runners wore white feather caps and announced their arrival with the trumpet call of a conch shell. . . ."

I could see it all in my mind's eye. Wildflowers in hues of yellow, purple, and orange dancing in the morning mist. A crystalline snow-white path that seemed to reach to the clouds leading to Machu Picchu, my personal Brigadoon. I forgot about my exhaustion as the dusty, shale-strewn trail beneath my feet was totally transformed. Inch by inch, Manolo painted verbal pictures of rulers and runners, powerful empires and ancient mysteries of a people who worshipped mountains and fervently protected themselves from ghosts. People who were not so different from myself.

As one who called the Maker of mountains "Father," I'd spent way too many years running from ghosts. The "me" I'd pictured in my mind was nothing but an apparition. It was conjured from words, lies I'd held onto so long that they sounded like truth. "You're unlovable. Fat. Ugly. Ordinary. Insignificant. Stupid. Worthless. Weak."

"Strong. Precious. Wise. Wonderful. Beautiful. Talented. Treasured. Redeemed. Loved more than you will ever know." God's truth called clearly to somewhere deep inside of me. My history was as ancient as the Incas. God's words were more solid, and eternal, than the mountain on which this Royal Road was built.

Manolo's voice, God's promises, and my own thoughts tumbled together as I continued to practice the "walk of the patient one," step after tiptoed step. Surprisingly soon, my dusty boots crested the summit. There I caught my first glimpse of the vista on the other side. It took my breath away even more than the altitude. What first appeared to be a band of clouds turned out to be hundreds of white stone steps built into the side of the mountain. Their descent seemed almost vertical, leading down to a plateau Manolo referred to as the Valley of Ghosts. But for me, at last, there was not a ghost in sight.

I surveyed the valley below and then the rocky path that led up the peak on the opposite side. It was only one of the two remaining summits we would climb before dinner that night. My eyes filled with tears, as they had so often during this trip. But this time they overflowed from a fresh spring of joy. I felt so free. So alive. So grateful to be where I was. To be who I was.

"This is the best day of my life!" I exclaimed to my girlfriend, quickly adding that my wedding day and the births of my two children were obviously exempt.

"That's what I like about you," she replied. "You're one of the only people I know who could lose their breakfast along the trail and less than an hour later make a statement like that."

She was right. I liked that about me too. As a matter of fact, I liked a lot of things about me.

After a bottle of water and a brief rest, I turned my back on Dead Woman's Pass. She'd lived up to her name. Someone had died along the way. Someone I had convinced myself I was. But someone God had never created me to be.

As I began to sidestep my way down the steep stone steps, I found myself once again watching my feet. One dusty purple boot in front of the other. But they seemed lighter now, almost as though they were dancing. *Here I am, Fred Astaire dancing down the Inca stairs.* . . . I felt the little girl inside suppress a giggle. I sure liked her taste in shoes.

> *I look up to the mountains—does my help come from*
> *there? My help comes from the LORD, who made the*
> *heavens and the earth!*
> Psalm 121:1 (NLT)

PERSONAL JOURNEY

HAVE you had a Dead Woman's Pass experience in life, physically, emotionally, or spiritually? How did you come away changed? If you're still struggling up the mountain, spend some time talking to God about how you can practice the "walk of the patient one" in this area of your life.

HAVE you ever wished you could walk someone else's path in life other than your own? If so, whose and why?

HOW can comparing your own personal journey with the journeys of others hinder you from truly accepting and enjoying who God created you to be?

READ Psalm 139:1–16 aloud. Ask God to show you the wonder of the precious and priceless, unique creation called *you.*

ARE there any "ghosts" conjured from lies that are following you around? Talk to God about them. Ask Him to help you exorcise them from your life with His truth. If there are any specific verses of Scripture God brings to mind, write them down on an index card. Read them aloud each morning until they are firmly planted in your mind.

Journey Toward . . .
WORSHIP

Williams,

Arizona

I opened the car door, stepping from air-conditioned comfort into a dry, desert wind. My sister and I weren't going anywhere. At least not right now. The only consolation seemed to be that neither was anyone else. A line of cars quickly accumulated behind us, sunglass-clad drivers peering out of open windows, inquisitive passengers poking up from sunroofs. All of us, craning our necks to see what could possibly be holding us up at a time like this.

I stopped, my feet momentarily forgetting how to move. Surely, I had stumbled onto holy ground. The quiet whispers surrounding us ceased.

Ahead of us lay a vast wasteland of automotive acceptance. Engines were turned off. Coolers were opened. Drivers and passengers alike stood beside their motionless vehicles, desperately trying to cool themselves with makeshift fans of fast-food bags or well-worn road maps. Kansas chatted with California. Arizona laughed with North Dakota. Kids of all ages, colors, and income brackets filled the sandy shoulder of the two-lane highway, playing tag, collecting rocks, comparing with newfound friends how many miles they'd traveled since dawn.

This scene all seemed oddly serene. No honking. No angry glares or impatient outbursts. More like old friends casually chatting over a Sunday barbecue than strangers thrown together by the inconvenience of road construction. Must be our common destination, I thought. After all, the road led to only one place—a worship service unparalleled anywhere else in the world. At least, that's what I'd heard.

I knew people who came here year after year. But as for me, I was a first-timer. A novice. A newbie. Expectant, anxious, perhaps even a bit skeptical. The truth is, I really wanted to be "wowed." However, at this point, I'd settle for being moved. Even a little.

In the distance, I saw the line of cars ahead of me begin inching forward. I slid back into the driver's seat, cranked up the air-conditioning, and joined the slow crawl toward the parking lot. Twenty minutes later we were greeted with a fistful of handouts from a gentleman hurrying cars through the front gate. "It starts at 6:37," he said with an air of urgency. "6:37! Don't be late!"

Pulling into the first available parking space, my sister and I quickly grabbed our jackets from the backseat. It seemed a ridiculous precaution on this sweltering day, but we'd heard the rumors. We wanted to be prepared, to keep any distractions to a minimum.

People streamed in from every direction, steps hurried, voices noticeably hushed. We joined the countless other latecomers, surging forward together as if we were a massive wave being pulled toward an inevitable shore. My sister gently nudged me toward the left. "It's quieter over here, less crowded," she said with the voice of experience. It was 6:35.

As we rounded the final curve, the massive sanctuary came into view. I stopped, my feet momentarily forgetting how to move. Surely, I had stumbled onto holy ground. The quiet whispers surrounding us ceased. My sister assertively guided me toward our front row seats. It was 6:37.

Never before, at least not in my experience, had silence so eloquently shouted God's name. It came in a chorus of color, from soft ginger to warm butterscotch, burnt sienna, and flaming auburn. Tones of cappuccino swirled with espresso. Layers of ocher and amber—alive—fluidly changing shade and hue before my eyes. As the warm tones began to cool, tiers of cobalt and plum melted into velvet indigos. Shadows caught in a slow waltz danced to the music of light and rhythm of time.

Then, unexpectedly, my perspective shifted. In my mind, what was once sky became sea. I was awash in the soft turquoise of early twilight—as seen from the ocean floor. The illusion made me involuntarily gasp for air, shuddering at the eerie sensation that giant creatures of the deep might appear out of the shadows at any moment.

This had been the reality, once upon a time. After all, God had used water as His paintbrush to create this Grand Canyon. The fossils of aquatic life were still here, telling the tale of a time gone by. Proclaiming God's attention to detail and His artist's eye. Speaking loudly to anyone who would listen. And tonight, thousands would hear.

Many of them wouldn't realize that it was Someone—not somewhere—that had called them to the canyon. But, they still came. Beckoned by God's glory. Drawn by His majesty. Led by their innate longing to worship at God's throne. Their hearts knew the truth, even if their minds could not yet accept it as fact.

As the last glimmer of sunlight faded from view, someone began to clap. Others joined in the chorus, one last outburst of spontaneous worship for the Ancient of Days. The applause echoed off the canyon walls, leaving the rocks alive with praise even after we'd turned our feet toward home.

> *Far and wide they'll come to a stop; they'll stare in awe, in wonder. Dawn and dusk take turns calling, "Come and worship."*
> Psalm 65:8 (*The Message*)

PERSONAL JOURNEY

CONSIDER a time when you were drawn to spontaneously worship God outside of a church-related activity. What was it that drew you to Him? In what way(s) did you worship Him?

WHY do you think God tells us to worship Him? What does worship do for God? For us?

IF people choose not to worship God, the desire to worship "something" doesn't go away. Name a few things people worship instead of God.

READ Psalm 84:10. How can travel draw us into God's court? How can it also be used to distract us from entering it?

WHEREVER you are right now, enter God's court. Spend some time worshipping Him.

Gubbio,

Italy

S now White gone bad—that's who Saint Ubaldo reminded me of. He was all decked out in a clear-glass coffin. Intricately embroidered golden threads adorned the folds of his snow-white robes. Gilt bronze fittings embellished each corner of his transparent tomb. And as the morning light filtered through the chapel's stained glass windows, the whole scene glistened like a fractured fairy tale. As I gazed up at

When it came crashing down onto the cobblestones of the piazza, people scrambled for pieces of the shattered pottery, rumored to be good luck charms. But still, no race.

him, on display perched high atop a towering marble pedestal, I found it far too easy to picture myself as one of the seven dwarfs in mourning. But I bet no one would be tempted to kiss those lips—or what was left of them.

Considering he died in the middle of the twelfth century, I had to admit it was pretty amazing Saint Ubaldo was in as good a shape as he was. Apparently the guy suffered from some bizarre type of oozing skin disease that mummified his body after death. I questioned whether this "miracle" of preservation was really an improvement over the usual bare-bones finale. The skin on Saint Ubaldo's face was stretched as taut as a size 4 swimsuit would be on my size 14 body. Not to mention the fact that he was a leathery burnished orange. Sleeping Beauty, Ubaldo was not.

I wondered how kids who attended the Basilica of Saint Ubaldo ever paid attention to the sermon on Sunday. I know what I was like as a kid attending Catholic Mass with my mom. I remember one nun explaining that the candle burning over the altar meant God was present. All through Mass I'd watch that candle, fighting the urge to run up to the front, vault over the Communion rail, and blow it out. I wanted to see what would happen if God was suddenly gone. I can't imagine where my mind would have wandered had there been a bona fide dead body right there in front of me every Sunday.

But now I hadn't come to attend mass, or even ogle Saint Ubaldo, though I guess he was considered the guest of honor at today's festivities. Now I was ready to witness the *Corsa dei Ceri*, the "Race of the Candles," one of two major feast days here in Gubbio, Italy. I'd heard that the other celebration involved crossbows. Candlesticks didn't sound half as exciting as lethal weapons. That is, until I saw them. These were no beeswax tapers. They were massive wooden pillars, carved into the shape of two eight-sided prisms stacked one on top of the other. These candlesticks on steroids rose about 10 feet tall and weighed almost 700 pounds.

From a distance, they resembled a sci-fi horror flick where giant killer ants walk on their hind legs, towering above a crowd of defenseless civilians. Only the legs of these ants were groups of ten men, trying to balance their colossal "ectoskeletons" on a platform they carried on their shoulders attached to a framework of wooden poles. I guess if Saint Ubaldo could remind me of Snow White, then these could be construed as candles. But it was the "wicks" that really grabbed my attention.

Atop each of the three *ceri* was a figure about 2½ feet tall. A knowledgeable local explained to me that one was Saint George, another Saint Anthony, and the last the legendary Saint Ubaldo (who looked much better, albeit shorter, than he did in the basilica). In the Corsa dei Ceri, each saint represents a different guild of workers: George is the patron of merchants and artisans; Anthony, the patron of farmers; and Ubaldo, the patron of masons. Once the race begins, people root for the patron saint of the profession they're most closely associated with. Since I'd heard Saint Anthony is also considered the patron saint of lost items and travelers, I decided to cheer him on toward victory. The next time the airlines lost my luggage, maybe I could call in a favor.

The noontime bell tolled through the medieval Palazzo dei Consoli. The *ceraioli,* or candle bearers, worked together to raise the top-heavy insect tapers to their shoulders. The three ceri wobbled and swayed as they rose, threatening to topple right over onto the sea of onlookers below. I was all set for excitement. Ready to run with the ceri. Ready to cheer with the crowd. But first, a pitcher of water was poured on the candlesticks, in spite of the fact that there was absolutely no risk of fire from these ceri. Then, the empty ceramic pitcher was thrown into the air. When it came crashing down onto the cobblestones of the piazza, people scrambled for pieces of the shattered pottery, rumored to be good luck charms. But still, no race.

Word on the street was that the official Corsa dei Ceri didn't begin until 6:00 P.M. I struggled to put my adrenaline on hold and enjoy the novelty of "now." Now was the time for anticipation—and for watching the slow procession of ceri through Gubbio's winding streets, rocky roads that hugged the side of Mount Ingino. Flowers were offered. Blessings bestowed. Pottery shards haggled over. But there was no running, no potential toppling, no ecstatic cheering. This race was beginning to feel like the "race" of my own life. A series of starts and stops. Adrenaline pumping with expectancy. Then, days spent plodding along at the pace of a snail with lead shoes.

At present, the bubbling adrenaline and the lead-footed gastropod were battling it out for supremacy in my life. In a few short weeks, I'd be back in the United States. For ten months I'd been a student in Florence, Italy. For ten months I'd stumbled over Italian verbs, tripped over unfamiliar customs, and found myself tangled up in all the emotions that come with being a foreigner, an outsider, an alien in a land I couldn't call my own.

Even with God I found myself feeling a bit like a "foreigner." Just three years earlier, I'd been running a race headed nowhere. A race toward trying to win the approval of others, trying to find Mr. Right (or even Mr. That'll Do), trying to find significance and joy and a diet that would leave me feeling beautiful. Trying to make it through life on my own.

But for the last three years I'd chosen to run a different kind of race, one where I tried to follow in the footsteps of Jesus. Some days He felt as close as my heartbeat. On others, my prayers seemed to echo back unanswered from the walls of my room. I was still trying to win the approval of others—only now those "others" included the God of the universe. While there were moments marked by victory, peace, and joy, there seemed to be weeks where the race of life left me feeling even more exhausted than when I was plodding along alone.

I was tired of what felt like false starts, dead-ends, and U-turns. It was time for somebody, anybody, to get out there and win. Maybe that's why I was so excited for those candlesticks to get a move on.

I was desperate for a taste of victory, even if it came secondhand.

When the church bells finally tolled 6:00, my adrenaline responded like Seabiscuit at the sound of a starter pistol. The candlesticks were on the run! Encouragement thundered from the sidelines as the crowds spilled down the village's roller coaster-sloped streets. The uneven stone walls of centuries-old dwellings echoed with the sound of different languages, as visitors and locals alike cheered on their favored team. Atop the swaying ceri, the miniature saints bobbed left and right, looking like uncoordinated toddlers trying to run uphill after an errant kite. Below, the ceraioli noticeably struggled beneath their uneven load. As they tired, a fresh crew of ceraioli transferred the weight of the wooden bars to their own shoulders.

Above the surging crowd, I saw the black robes of Saint Anthony swaying wildly in the evening breeze. He was closely followed by the ceri of Saint George, robed in cerulean blue, and Saint Ubaldo, cloaked in sunflower yellow. As the candlesticks passed, the crowd fell into step behind the last team. The spectators followed the ceraioli uphill, undoubtedly thankful they bore only backpacks, purses, and shopping bags overflowing with souvenirs, instead of almost 700 pounds of wobbling saint.

By the time the 2½-mile course through the streets neared the finish line, the race had slowed to a sweaty crawl. Before us lay the final lung-taxing ascent to the Basilica of Saint Ubaldo, the church where my own day's journey had begun. High above the shoulder-to-shoulder crowd, my black-robed hero was still visibly in the lead. My heart pounded with exhaustion and anticipation. Knowing that certain victory was only minutes away felt good. However, I couldn't help but empathize with poor Saint Ubaldo bringing up the rear. There would always be a place in my heart for underdogs. So often, I felt like one of them. But right now, I was in the lead. Celebration was close at hand. I was winning, as surely as if I carried that saint on my very own shoulders. The words of the British rock group Queen resounded in my head, *"WE are the champions . . ."*

That's when the impossible happened. Saint Anthony not only stopped moving forward, he pulled off to the side of the street. Then, runner-up Saint George followed suit. And Saint Ubaldo? He continued heading uphill, slow, but steady. As Anthony and George stood immobile on the sidelines, Ubaldo bypassed them both, entering the doors of the basilica and finishing the race in first place. I stood stone-still in stunned silence as the surrounding crowd went wild with celebratory cheers.

"I don't get it! What happened?" I shouted above the roar to a friend standing nearby. "Saint Anthony was in the lead!"

"Didn't you hear?" she yelled back. "Saint Ubaldo always wins."

"What kind of race is that?" I demanded.

What kind of race indeed. . . .

Decades passed before I came to see the real beauty behind the race of the candlesticks, before I understood that when God "wins," so do I. For years, my definition of victory was having life turn out the way I wanted it to. When I lived in Italy as a college student, almost 30 years ago, I was running a double-minded race—one foot on God's path and one foot on my own. I was trying to please God while at the same time pleading with Him to write the story of my life according to my own personal outline. Instead of seeking God, I was seeking an eternal good luck charm.

But God is not a talisman, a shard of "lucky" pottery snatched up before the Corsa dei Ceri begins. And I'm not simply another face in the crowd who tries to follow God by running along behind Him, trying my best to keep up, and every so often being allowed the privilege of glimpsing a "real" saint under glass or from a distance. God calls me—common, everyday, ordinary me—a saint. He says I'm a "holy one" set apart to run a race that's guaranteed to lead straight home to Him. My victory is certain, even when it may not look like I'm in the lead. It doesn't matter how fast I run. It doesn't matter when the load God's given me to carry bobbles a bit along the way. All that matters is that I persevere along the course He's set before me.

Over the course of my life so far, this race has taken me up steep slopes, down into gullies, and over uneven, unfamiliar terrain more often than it has led me through placid, peaceful meadows. It's so much more of a daring adventure than I ever would have scripted for myself. But I never run it alone. God is not out in front, but by my side, encouraging me every step of the way.

Reminiscent of the Corsa dei Ceri, Scripture tells me that as I run I'm surrounded by a "great cloud of witnesses." Saints are cheering me on from the sidelines. They are people who have gone before me, saints I have loved and lost in this life, but who are waiting at heaven's finish line for my arrival. Saints whom I've not yet met, but who are bound to me through our mutual family tree of faith. Saints who have finished the race God set before them. Victors, one and all.

Who knows? Maybe Anthony, George, and Ubaldo are among them, cheering me on, shouting from the sidelines, "Forget about being first. Focus on being faithful!"

> *Since we are surrounded by such a great cloud of witnesses, let us throw off everything that hinders and the sin that so easily entangles, and let us run with perseverance the race marked out for us.*
> Hebrews 12:1 (NIV)

PERSONAL JOURNEY

HOW does it feel to call yourself a saint, to see yourself as someone who is set apart and holy? Do you have difficulty imagining others follow God in this way?

IF Saint Ubaldo were alive today, what do you feel the two of you might have in common?

READ Hebrews 12:1–3. Is there anything hindering you from running the race you believe God has set before you? If so, what is one thing you can do to help "untangle" yourself from it?

DO you ever view God as a good luck charm or a vending machine where you put in your prayer and expect God's answer to pop out according to your own personal specifications? What's the danger of picturing God in this way?

FIND three Scripture verses that deal with the topic of victory. Does God's definition of victory differ at all from your own? Ask God to help you better understand what it means to be victorious in this life and the next.

Journey Toward . . .
HEALING

Colorado Springs,
Colorado

D eath—like a slap in the face from a God I thought I knew—caught me off-guard. Stunned, I wandered through the house, accomplishing nothing. Picking up a dish from breakfast, I absentmindedly scraped the egg into the sink. Then I set the plate back on the counter, too distracted to place it in the dishwasher. I wandered aimlessly into the family room, looking for something to do. Something to give me

I ventured off the path, trampling stray weeds with my feet. Suddenly, I stopped. I backed up.

purpose. Something to set my feet firmly back on solid ground.

Brent's unexpected death filled my head with a fog that wouldn't lift. He'd been rock climbing with his best friend and other men he cared deeply about. Of course, Brent cared deeply about a lot of people. One of them was a close friend of mine who'd spent the last five years in Brent's counseling office working her way through great valleys of heartache. Where would people like my friend go now—people who were already overwhelmed by the pain of life, gasping for air as they tried to keep their heads above water in their very personal rushing torrents of grief? What about Brent's wife? His sons? His best friend? Me?

What were you thinking, God? I prayed for Brent almost every day. For wisdom, for honesty and integrity, for protection . . . What protection did You offer? Is this how You show Your love to those who are faithful? To those who risk loving others wholeheartedly? To those who dare to follow You?

The tears were back. I quickly jammed my sunglasses onto my face, grabbed my house keys, and headed out the door. I couldn't stand being inside any longer. It was too quiet, making it too easy to think. Too easy to feel.

With quick, angry steps, I made my way toward the familiar greenway that wove a path through the neighborhood. It was the same path I walked every morning. The path where I prayed for Brent and so many others like him. Usually this was a path of peace, one that led me toward worship and praise. Today it felt like a reminder of betrayal. Of a God who had not come through when someone I cared for needed Him most. Head down, my hands tightly clenched, hot tears burning salty tracks down my cheeks, I plowed forward. Like an armored tank intentionally rolling over a bed of fragile seedlings, I ventured off the path, trampling stray weeds with my feet.

Suddenly, I stopped. I backed up. Tentatively, I stepped forward again, closing my eyes and taking a deep, deliberate breath. Lilacs . . . The sweet scent filled my lungs, and my soul, with a heady perfume. People speak of certain scents as being intoxicating. Quite the contrary, the fragrance from this one unassuming lilac bush didn't leave me feeling drunk, but sober. I was alive, awake, clearheaded for the first time in days.

Eyes still closed, I breathed in once more. I felt as though I'd spent the last three days underwater, holding my breath since Brent's death. The lilac's invisible veil of perfume was only discernible in one small spot. So I just stood there, filling myself with what felt like a whiff of life.

The fragrance transported my thoughts back to a garden in France. The garden wasn't part of a grand castle or chateau. Not listed in guidebooks or mentioned on bus tours. Merely a row of rose bushes lining a walkway at a highway rest stop. Other countries would have been content with an arrow on a green metal sign pointing the way to the restrooms. But this was France. And in France, nothing is so insignificant that it cannot be presented in a beautiful way.

Each plant had been placed with artistic intention. The blossoms on the line of rose bushes progressed from deep blood red to baby-cheek pink to fresh-picked apricot and pressed-linen white. The winding, gravel path was edged with the flowers' gradual transition of color. The gentle perfume that accompanied each variety of rose changed subtly along the way as well. Subtle, but discernible, and indescribably delightful. Like the lilac bush, the scent of the roses had stopped me in my tracks that day as well.

I remembered calling out to my husband, wanting him to join me among the roses, to share in my unexpected discovery. But he just shook his head and wiped his watery eyes. Hay fever compelled him to remain on the asphalt walkway below.

So, I savored the sweetness of that moment in France alone. As I did now in my own backyard. Or so I thought at first. But in that brief moment, something changed. My fog of grief lifted as unexpectedly as it had appeared. Like a magic wardrobe filled with fur coats, this common lilac bush was a secret passageway. But instead of leading me to Narnia it led me straight into the majesty and mystery of God's presence. He was there. Seemingly closer than He had ever been, holding me in His arms and whispering in my ear, *I've been waiting for you. Shall we take a walk together?*

Stunned into silence, my tears and questioning ceased. Who am I to turn down an invitation from God?

Feeling as if I were Adam strolling in the Garden of Eden, I walked and talked with God that day in a way words can't begin to describe. There was no lightning flash, no audible voice emanating from a burning lilac bush. Yet something radically changed—both inside and out. I noticed details, beauty along the path I'd walked every morning for years. Miracles I'd casually passed by before, unseeing. . . .

Tiny purple wildflowers budding among common weeds. Wild sage, its leaves covered with a soft, silver silk that I simply had to bend down and touch. Miniature cacti, looking delightfully out of place against the backdrop of the snow-dusted Colorado Rockies. A field of dry grass dancing to the rhythm of a late spring breeze. Shadows playing tag as songbirds supplied a more than Grammy-worthy sound track for the early morning production.

Every detail, every color, every texture, every breeze, and every ray of sunshine was created by the hand of an Artist who knows no equal. Here I was, casually walking through a gallery of wonders, with the Creator acting as curator. And it was not only the natural beauty that caught my eye, it was the people I saw along the way. The middle-aged woman walking her dog. The glassy-eyed driver barreling along Research Boulevard. The towheaded toddlers giggling in the playground. With each new face I saw, I could almost hear God whisper, *I love that one . . . and that one . . . and that one. . . . Look at her smile . . . his eyes . . . their abandon at play.* Each individual was a brand-new canvas, lovingly created with an Artist's eye.

Everything and everyone seemed more precious, more sacred than ever before. Leave it to God to fashion a key to hidden treasure out of something as scorned as grief. Yet here I was, glimpsing God's gallery as though for the very first time. Feeling the first caresses of healing. Feeling humbled and blessed and hopeful and loved. Feeling overcome with wonder and wholeheartedly alive.

The author of Ecclesiastes was right. There is a time for every season under heaven. Winter and spring. Laughter and tears. Work and rest. Season after changing season . . . My season of mourning had not yet come to an end, but my heart confirmed what my head believed. God was still in control and there was a plan. Even if I didn't understand it all.

But, there was another truth I could not ignore. A "madman" was loose in the gallery. He'd slashed countless numbers of priceless canvases, trampled on the delicate pottery, spray-painted graffiti on the sculptured marble. He'd left both nature, and humanity, looking like the Venus de Milo. Beautiful, but flawed. No longer complete.

Brent's death was just one sign of his presence. For every Grand Canyon, there was a Killing Field. For every Matterhorn, an Auschwitz. The image of God obscured by the depravity of evil. Yet, God's image remained, calling to me. Drawing me ever closer to Him. Healing me in unexpected ways. Leading me on journeys I'd never dare set foot on alone. Reminding me that there is a place where there will be no more tears. But I'm not there yet.

Day by day, I continue to walk with God through His gallery of wonders with my eyes and heart wide open, ready for anything. Like Job, whose heartache led him to question God—and whose only reply was *Look at the works of My hands and remember who I am*—I found even grief can be a gifted teacher in the hands of a gracious God. After all, if God can use a lilac bush to heal a broken heart, I trust He can use a broken person like me to embrace a broken world.

> *He heals the brokenhearted and binds up*
> *their wounds.*
> Psalm 147:3 (NIV)

PERSONAL JOURNEY

RECALL a season of grief in your life. On what kind of journey did it lead you? If you invited God to join you on this journey, did He lead you anywhere unexpected?

EVEN "Jesus wept" (John 11:35) over the death of His friend Lazarus—right before He raised him from the dead. What do Jesus's tears teach you about grief, and about God?

READ Romans 1:20. Consider a few of God's wondrous "works of art." What do they reveal to you about God's character? What do you think this verse in Romans means when it says people are "without excuse"?

HOW has the "madman" in God's gallery vandalized the masterpiece of you? How is God's restoration process progressing in your life? Talk to God about this ongoing process, asking Him to help you sort out what is His part and what is yours.

TAKE a walk through God's gallery with your eyes and heart wide open. Let your journey lead you toward worshipping the Artist behind it all.

Journey Toward . . .
FAITH

Bruges,
Belgium

O nce upon a time, there was a mother who took her beautiful daughter to a fairy-tale village. Shop windows were filled with chocolate formed into fanciful shapes. Swans drifted along a lazy canal, which crisscrossed clean-swept cobbled streets. Like a child's toy soldiers, the caramel-colored stone buildings—topped with rosy red roof hats—stood at attention, side by side. They made a nearly seamless curving wall

Except for being carefully hidden during the two world wars, the relic has remained in Bruges's Basilica of the Holy Blood every since, unopened.

that formed the neighborhoods and town squares of Bruges. Did I mention the $6.00 lemonade?

"You're going to lick every last melting ice cube out of that glass!" I said to my daughter under my breath. Katrina looked back at me with a guilty smile. We knew our café on the church square was far beyond the borders of the land of free refills. I picked up my own glass and downed the last tiny drops of a beverage some elf must have spun out of gold.

Despite a lunch tab fit for a king, so far our day truly felt as if we'd stepped into the pages of a storybook. Right before noon, we'd descended from the viewing platform atop the medieval bell tower (a mere 732-step round-trip) right into the path of an oncoming parade. Unaware that Ascension Day is one of Bruges's most internationally acclaimed annual celebrations, or even that Ascension Day happened to fall on the one day we happened to be in town, we found ourselves face-to-face with crusaders on horseback. They were followed by fair maidens in gowns tipped with handmade lace and cherry-cheeked boys carrying the banners of ancient guilds. A wide spectrum of assorted historical characters passed inches away from where we stood. My sister and her husband who were traveling with us, both professional travel photographers, couldn't believe our luck. Their camera lenses were clicking away as steadily as horses' hooves on the cobblestones.

I was intrigued by the spectacle. But truthfully, I'd never given much thought to Ascension Day. I knew it was celebrated in honor of the day Jesus "ascended" to heaven, 40 days after He rose from the grave. And I guess if I'd been there with the disciples that day, I'd have felt differently. Watching someone I love die, return to life, and then leave again by disappearing into the clouds certainly would have been an event I'd celebrate year after year.

But this parade was recalling more than Jesus's return to heaven. It was a reenactment of the Count of Flanders's return to Bruges after the Second Crusade carrying a holy cargo: a vial of Christ's blood. As the story goes, Joseph of Arimathea, the man who asked Pilate for Jesus's body so it could be prepared for burial, preserved His blood after washing it from the body. A fragment of cloth containing a few drops of this mixture of blood and water was later placed into a rock crystal vial. Then the vial was put inside a glass cylinder and sealed with two golden lids cast in the shape of crowns. The count was presented with the relic in Jerusalem in recognition of his contributions during the Crusades. In turn, the count presented this vial of "Holy Blood" to the people of Bruges in 1150. Except for being carefully hidden during the two world wars, the relic has remained in Bruges's Basilica of the Holy Blood every since, unopened.

To me, the story seemed like a chapter out of *The Da Vinci Code*. Fiction. Fantasy. A fairy-tale plot. But when the church beside the café where we'd finished our lunch opened up, and we were presented with a rare opportunity to view the vial of Holy Blood for ourselves, there seemed to be no other reasonable choice than to go and take a look.

After the glaring midday sun on the square, walking into the basilica left me fumbling for a moment in the dark. The richly painted vaulted ceilings, arches, and murky-toned artwork held an almost stiflingly heavy air of reverence, imposing silence with all the authority of a stern-faced librarian. A liturgical chant cut through the quiet. The muffled steps of a small procession of altar boys accompanied a priest to a side altar. Here the priest took the relic of the Holy Blood in his hands, gave it a tender kiss, and then held it high for all to see.

People lined up for a chance to draw closer. To see Christ's blood with their own eyes. To kiss this holy relic with their own lips. The scene brought back memories of standing in line to see the Shroud of Turin years before. I was one of 3½ million people who waited for hours to spend less than a minute in front of a piece of frayed cloth. The shroud was displayed in a nitrogen-filled case behind bulletproof glass, which spoke to both the controversy behind the artifact and to the miraculous claims of the God-man whose image it supposedly held. As I surveyed the likeness of a man's haggard features, I wondered, *Could I really be looking at the face of my Lord?*

I came to the conclusion that it really didn't matter. If it was real, cool. If it was a hoax—a fairy tale unknowingly perpetuated by those who deeply wanted something tangible to help them hold tightly to a so-often intangible God—I understood. But my faith never had been based on what I could see. So truth or fairy tale, a shroud or a vial of blood held little power to inspire my awe or reverence. I reserved that for God Himself.

"Aren't you going to go?" my brother-in-law whispered. He knew Katrina and I believed in God, something he didn't profess.

"No thanks," I whispered back. "Seeing it from here is fine." I couldn't join the line of those who kissed the vial with such fervent respect. I felt as though my simple curiosity would mock their sincerity. I knew we loved the same Lord. But I also believed that "holy blood" flowed through my changed heart because of Christ's sacrifice. I believed I carried God's image more certainly than the Shroud of Turin. My own life was a "relic" authenticated by faith.

But I wondered what the scene looked like through my brother-in-law's eyes. Did he see God as a fantasy, nothing more than a fairy tale? A nice story used to comfort the kids on a cold, stormy night? Did he put the legend of the Holy Blood on the same scale as that of Calvary? Did he see anything in my life or my daughter's that made him wonder, *what if?* Why had faith taken hold in my heart and not his?

I had to admit my own faith was far from neat and tidy. It refused to fit into the concise little box of logic and understanding. Some things I believed did sound like fairy tales . . . water turning into wine, a storm being calmed with mere words, people rising from the dead. Who could understand and explain everything God says and does? But God's presence and purpose answered more questions in my life than it raised. So I found myself falling in love and following a God I couldn't see. But I hadn't yet come to the end of the story, to the moment when all the loose ends tie together, to the moment when the true identity of the King becomes apparent to all. Until then, all I knew how to do was keeping moving forward in faith.

As the line to view the Holy Blood grew, my brother-in-law, sister, daughter, and I made our way out of the dim sanctuary and back into the bright light of the square. It was nearing time for us to catch our bus. The lively animation of our conversation earlier in the day seemed more subdued, even a bit awkward. Perhaps we were just tired. Or, perhaps, the mixture of faith and fairy tales we'd encountered that day just needed some time to settle in our brains. We needed time to think, to sort, to evaluate, to ask ourselves, *what if?*

We quietly retraced our steps back through town. Past a sculpture of Neptune rising from the sea, fashioned entirely of chocolate. Past women rhythmically shuffling dozens of bobbins of thread, in what looked like methodical chaos, to create handmade lace. Past horse-drawn carts and cloistered gardens. Past the narrow stone arch of Blind Donkey Alley. Back toward the real world, with its asphalt, billboards, car horns, and fast food. We made one stop along the way to purchase a box of chocolate seashells. A souvenir of our time in Bruges that disappeared almost as quickly as the fairy-tale atmosphere we left behind.

And so, did the mother and the beautiful daughter live happily ever after? Well, "happily" is so subjective. They had their good days and their bad days. And even a few $6.00 lemonades. But as for their "ever after," Jesus had made certain that was secure.

> *We walk by faith, not by sight.*
> 2 Corinthians 5:7 (NKJV)

PERSONAL JOURNEY

REGARDLESS of what you think about the actual authenticity of Bruges's Holy Blood or the Shroud of Turin, would you like them to be real? Why or why not?

WHAT impact do you think having irrefutable proof of God's existence would have on your faith? Read John 20:29. What do you think about what Jesus has to say?

WHY do you think God designed us to "walk by faith, not by sight"?

MARK 9:24 (NIV) says, "'I do believe. Help me overcome my unbelief.'" Can you relate to this man's prayer? What is one thing you have trouble believing about God? Why? How can doubt and faith coexist?

TURN the words of Mark 9:24 into your own prayer. Talk to God about how you can "walk by faith" more closely today—and how you can help others do the same.

Journey Toward . . .

WONDER

Montaña de Oro,
California

T he steep climb left us breathless. Quiet for the first time that day. That's probably the only reason we heard it; the sound of thousands of hands rubbing together in eager anticipation.

"Listen," I whispered. Like synchronized swimmers my sister and I stopped and cocked our heads.

"What is it?" we asked each other in unison. It was a question neither of us could answer. *Motorcycle hum? Insect*

That's when we heard it. The sound of something strangely surreal. We turned toward the noise and headed off into the unknown.

buzz? Distorted echo of crashing waves? Birds' mating grounds? The sound was so consistent, so foreign, so completely unidentifiable that there was only one thing we could do. Follow it. With the power of the Pied Piper, the mystical music drew Cindy and me off the trail deep into a eucalyptus grove nearby.

We'd spent the morning at my favorite beach, which was deserted as usual. Accessed only through a break in the brush barely visible from the park's main road, it was one of those "secret spots" whose location is selectively shared with trusted friends. That's why I brought Cindy. People call us sisters, but we're more like Siamese twins separated by 18 months. Unfortunately, for the last year we'd been separated by state lines. While I attended college on the central coast of California, Cindy worked on a ranch in Nevada. But not today. Today we were joined at the hip once more.

A blanket to sit on, pockets to hold seashells, and time to catch up on all the little nonessentials that so often go unsaid when you're struggling to keep up with long distance phone bills . . . we had everything we needed. Except for lunch. The sun that warmed our backs this fall morning was now almost directly overhead. It was time to hike back up to the car so we could head off in search of the perfect bowl of clam chowder.

That's when we heard it. The sound of something strangely surreal. We turned toward the noise and headed off into the unknown. Every hundred feet or so we'd pause, listen, reevaluate our direction, and readjust our course. We forgot our pursuit of chowder to search for who-knew-what.

As we drew closer to the source of the sound, its intensity grew— though intensity is such a strong word for such an understated resonant rustle. My mind jumped from one conclusion to the next . . . *Hive of killer bees? Static on car radio that's tumbled down a cliff? Secret generator for the nuclear power plant that lay on the other side of the mountain???* Creativity quickly turned my brainstorm into worry-driven anxiety, but my curiosity still outweighed my fear.

I paused, motionless, closed my eyes, and tried to focus solely on the sound.

That's when Elijah popped into my mind. Depressed, despondent, and afraid, the prophet was hiding out in a cave, waiting for the arrival of the God who'd promised He'd show up. Knowing no one could see the Almighty and live, Elijah undoubtedly waited while peeking through one almost closed eye—and listening with two very attentive ears.

First, Elijah heard the rush of a raging wind. It ripped rocks out of the mountainside, dashing them into gravel and dust. But Elijah did not find God in the wind. Then, Elijah heard the rumbling crack of an earthquake, cutting fissures into the ground on which he stood. But, Elijah did not find God in the earthquake. Next, the roar of a fire consuming the trees and brush nearby filled Elijah's anxious ears. Again, God was not in the fire. Then, came a gentle whisper. That's when all of the pieces fell into place. Elijah recognized the sound of God's voice at once and immediately covered his face with his cloak. God had shown up.

I knew the strange sound I was following wasn't an earthquake, a forest fire, or an errant wind. I also knew it wasn't the voice of God. Like Elijah, I was sure if I heard His gentle whisper, I'd recognize it at once. Yet something about this moment whispered, "God is near." My mind no longer jumped to conclusions. Instead, it basked in the anticipation of wonderful answers.

And those answers were close by. I could tell. I closed my eyes once more and listened. Prom dresses, thousands of them, brushing against one another. Ripples of taffeta, velvet, and silk adorned with satin ribbons, coarse netting, and crisp crinoline petticoats, slow dancing side-by-side in a crowded hall. That's what it was. That was the sound. The hands rubbing together in anxious anticipation had finished. The dance had begun.

"Look . . ." I opened my eyes in response to my sister's voice. Following her into an airy grove, my eyes confirmed what my ears had whispered was true. I was surrounded by dancing. Graceful twirls, dips, jetés, and pliés filled the air. Instead of adolescent girls, butterflies waltzed on sun-warmed wings. But these few hundred dancers were only the welcome chorus. In the middle of the grove stood a towering tree so thickly covered by clumps of leaves that they almost blocked out the sun. I took a closer look. The leaves were breathing. In and out, in and out, in and out . . . a warm-up routine before taking a turn on the floor. My "leaves" were wings, aching to fly.

Thousands upon thousands of monarch butterflies were layered over the tree's trunk and branches like a closet stuffed with gossamer gowns. Slowly the butterflies changed partners, allowing those on top to step aside for those beneath. During storms this routine offered them protection from the rain and cold, but today all the monarchs seemed to want was to have their solo in the sun.

If only I'd known my ordinary morning would become an extraordinary encounter, I would have brought a camera. Today, memory would have to serve as film, just as it had a year earlier when Cindy and I were driving to Santa Barbara. That morning we'd been talking animatedly—as usual—when a sudden onslaught of brake lights brought our conversation to a halt.

"Look!" we shouted in unison, pointing to a furry brown wave undulating beneath the cars in front of us.

"What is it?" we inquired of each other. That day it had been woolly bear caterpillars, migrating across the coastal freeway. We had to keep rolling, but gave empathetic screams out the open windows, shouting, "Move! Move! Move!" as our mammoth truck tires undoubtedly ended the journey of more caterpillars than we cared to consider. Today, our privileged glimpse into God's glorious gallery was decidedly less deadly. We lingered a while longer, enchanted by the joyful flutter.

Montaña de Oro . . . "Mountain of Gold." The park was named for the golden wildflowers that blanketed its hillsides each spring. But today that name spoke of countless golden wings. You'd think that after years of finding myself dumbstruck by the beauty, creativity, and outright audacity of God's world and His ways, I'd no longer be surprised when an ordinary day takes an extraordinary turn. But I'm a slow learner. That's why I need to learn from the Boy Scouts to "be prepared." We're living in a world of wonder. We may not find God in the wind, in the earthquake, or in the fire. But you never know when He'll show up. You might find Him in the gentle whisper of silky saffron wings.

Let Wilderness turn cartwheels,
Animals, come dance,
Put every tree of the forest in the choir—
An extravaganza before GOD as he comes.
Psalm 96:12–13 (*The Message*)

PERSONAL JOURNEY

PSALM 66:5 (*The Message*) says, "Take a good look at God's wonders—they'll take your breath away." Recall a time when God's wonders left you awestruck. What does that experience have to teach you about God's character, creativity, and power?

WHEN the Bible says God is *wonderful*, what does that mean to you? Does the word's meaning change at all in light of what you've just read?

GOD says that you are wonderfully made. What does that say about you and about your Creator?

ONLY the fifth generation of monarch butterflies migrate, so they are never led to their wintering site by memory or by butterflies that have traveled to that spot before. Name a few instinctive traits God has woven into your human design. Why do you think He did this?

FOR the next week, make a mental note each morning to take Job 37:14 (NIV) to heart: "Stop and consider God's wonders." At the end of the week, journal what you've learned about God as you've tried to be more attentive to the natural world that surrounds you.

Chiang Mai,
Thailand

N ow I knew what a lottery ball felt like. I bobbed wildly atop a flat wooden plank balanced on the rounded back of a very large elephant. I carefully weighed the risk of taking a photo. A piece of jute twine, already threatening to unravel, was the only safety belt in place to keep me from toppling off of my perch and onto the head of the young *mahout,* the Thai elephant trainer, who was riding below on

Here I was riding through the jungles of Thailand singing about the Blue Ridge Mountains and Shenandoah River.

the beast's shoulders. I doubted the twine had the strength to pull a tooth, let alone hold back the body weight of a premenopausal woman suddenly catapulted through the air by the jerky lurch of an elephant's gait as it slogged across a craggy creek bed.

But I've always been an adventurer at heart. So I removed the camera's lens cap with one hand as my calves tightly gripped the sandpaper sides of Big Bertha—or whatever the pachyderm's name happened to be. The mahout had repeated it to me when we began our ride, but it, along with the mahout's name and most of the other Thai words I'd heard so far, refused to form a repeatable syllable in my head. I could blame it on the heat, which was sweltering. I could blame it on my hearing, which at 45 was already starting to show signs of one too many rock concerts. But instead I chose to place the blame right where I felt it belonged: on God. After all, if it weren't for that whole Tower of Babel thing, the mahout and I could have been best friends by now, having carried on a coherent conversation for the last half hour, instead of lumbering along in silence.

I had picked up a few handy phrases during my two weeks in Thailand, such as *sawat di ka* and *khawp khun kha* ("hello" and "thank you"). But when I tried to use what I thought was the Thai word for "beautiful" to compliment a vendor on her handmade purses, she looked at me like I'd lost my mind. That's what happens when you have an alphabet of 44 consonants, 15 vowels, and five different tones in which syllables can be voiced. Our guide assured me that Thai was much easier to speak than it is to write. That cheered me up considerably.

Of course, I figured the Thai people found themselves at pretty much the same loss as I did. Written translations from Thai into English are like word puzzles, leaving readers struggling to decipher their intended meaning. A sign on a trail near the Kwai Noi River read, word-for-misspelled, misinterpreted-word: *The trail is embrassed of asphalt road, concreted road and well-forming red soil road, hugged by big threes and villages.* I wondered if being hugged by big "threes" was the cause of the trail's embarrassment. Or there was the T-shirt I purchased on the banks of the River Kwai which read, *The Bride over the River Kwai*. One little *g* really can make a big difference. However, my personal favorite was printed on the chair of a boat we'd taken for a ride down the Chao Phraya River in Bangkok. I believe its intent was to point out the location of our life jackets. It read: *Life savings under seat.*

Yes, the Tower of Babel was alive and well. And right now there was some babbling going on that I couldn't quite decipher. I could tell by the tone of his voice that the mahout was asking me a question; but since it didn't involve "thank you" or "hello," I was totally lost. Then I noticed young men hanging out of surrounding trees holding bunches of bananas. I watched the elephant passengers in front of me struggling to get a few baht (the local currency) out of their pockets to purchase a bunch of bananas. The mahout then handed the bananas to the elephant. Ah, a snack stop . . . Obviously the only answer to the mahout's question was yes. A happy elephant is a complacent elephant. I certainly didn't want a rogue on my hands. I still had at least 40 minutes to go on this lottery ball bounce through the jungle along the Mae Ping River.

Once the elephant was happy, the mahout seemed happier as well. We were told at the beginning of our ride that the relationship between a mahout and his elephants is almost like family, built up over years of working and training together. Certainly from my vantage point, Big Bertha and the young mahout who seemed so at home on her neck, appeared to be good friends. They didn't speak the same language and they seemed to have developed a relationship. Maybe we could too. I began to relax. Well, as much as a person can while living with the constant fear of pitching over the head of an elephant.

The trees above us formed a broken canopy tracing lacy shadows on the rich, red soil below. The Thai sky looked the same as I'd seen it every day of the trip so far—when it wasn't opened up pouring buckets of slate gray rain. It held a promise of blue, hidden behind layers of smoke, car exhaust, and low-lying clouds. As Bertha and her cargo ambled along, I heard occasional rustles in the leafy undergrowth. Probably snakes, lizards, and mice, I noted. Instantly, I tried to shake childhood memories of Dumbo rearing up at the sight of a tiny gray mouse.

Please, God, don't let me fall off this elephant and make an idiot of myself. At that moment, I found myself truly thankful that God invites us to pray about anything and everything. *Just grip with your ankles, sway with the flow, grip with your ankles, sway with the flow . . .* became my internal sound track. The mahout had his own external one.

It started off tentatively, a quiet little whistle under his breath. But it continued to grow, picking up volume and discernible melody. It was "Take Me Home, Country Roads" by John Denver, one of my favorite songs in high school. The album that the song was on inspired me to pick up a guitar and learn how to play. I couldn't speak Thai, but I did know the words to the song. My own self-confidence and I began an outwardly silent battle: *You can't just burst into song on the back of this elephant! What are people going to think? . . . But I want to communicate with my mahout and I can't speak Thai. Maybe a song will help. . . . You'll communicate all right! You'll announce to everyone that you're not only nuts, but tone-deaf. God, what do You think?*

I left my pride in the dust of Bertha's stride and opened my mouth. "Take me home, country roads . . ."

The whistling stopped and the mahout turned to look at me. A wide smile spread across his face. Then he turned back toward the Thai country road ahead and started over from the beginning. His whistling and my singing filtered through the trees toward the rest of my tour group. They looked around, whispered to one another, pointed fingers, but then seemed to quiet down and enjoy the free musical entertainment.

Here I was riding through the jungles of Thailand singing about the Blue Ridge Mountains and Shenandoah River. I didn't want this road to take me home. I liked where I was and who I was with. I couldn't pronounce his name, but I knew a bit about this mahout's heart. It was like mine. It enjoyed God's creation and His gift of music. I didn't need words to tell me that.

"John Denver!" my mahout announced proudly when we finished our duet. He gave me a thumbs-up. I applauded his whistling skills—and the fact that he could pronounce names that were not native to Thailand.

"Eric Clapton?" he questioned. He began whistling the tune to "Tears in Heaven."

"Would you know my name if I saw you in heaven?" I joined in. As I sang the words, I multitasked, conversing with God in prayer. *Maybe I would someday . . .* know this man's name in heaven, that is. God knew it, and could pronounce it, even if I couldn't. So, I asked God to make Himself known in this man's life. To bring people to him who would tell him about a God who not only loves him but understands Thai perfectly. A God who is able to translate both our deepest groans and heartfelt cries into the heavenly language of prayer. A God who calls Himself the Word. A God who can use any country's road to take us Home, to the place we belong.

> *The LORD your God is with you, he is mighty to save. He will take great delight in you, he will quiet you with his love, he will rejoice over you with singing.*
> Zephaniah 3:17 (NIV)

PERSONAL JOURNEY

WHAT does "Preach the gospel at all times; if necessary, use words" (Saint Francis of Assisi) mean to you? Do you think it's valid advice?

WHAT are ways you can communicate your love, and God's love, to others without using words? Find two Scripture verses that support this idea. Use a Bible concordance to help you.

WHAT are ways God has communicated His love to you without using words?

PEOPLE are the only one of God's creations with the ability to use words to communicate. That's one unique way we reflect His image. How does the way you use words present a positive or a poor reflection of God's character? What does Matthew 12:35–37 have to say about this?

WHAT part does music play in your life and in your relationship with God? Step out of your comfort zone for a moment and "Sing to the LORD a new song" (Psalm 96:1 NIV). Don't worry about rhythm, rhyme, or even pitch. Sing what's on your heart, even if your song only comes out in a whisper.

Mittersill,

Austria

The bus driver pointed to a bright star in the midnight sky. "Schloss Mittersill," he announced. I squinted my tired eyes in the direction of the twinkling light. A castle, not a star, awaited me. Cloaked in the heavy velvet of night and sedated by exhaustion, my mind refused to record the details of my arrival in any way that resembled an accurate image. Instead, blurred snapshots of a cobbled path beneath an arched gateway,

The castle grounds on which we stood had risen from the ashes. It had been the home to depravity, but now held a chorus of praise.

massive wooden doors, a dimly lit narrow hallway, and the muffled echo of snow boots on stone floors tumbled together in random order. Before I fell into bed, my mind was already dreaming.

My surroundings came clearly into focus along with the all-too-persistent early morning sun. Trying to convince myself I was still in bed, I wrapped a quilt around my shoulders and headed to the window. The louvered shutters opened with a quiet "click." In the stark stillness of the dawn the sound was enough to scatter the birds from the surrounding trees. But everything else laid frozen, unmoving, postcard perfect.

The town below looked like a miniature Christmas village. A gauzy layer of mist hung over the valley, pierced by a shiny church steeple. Sugar-frosted roofs topped gingerbread houses. Sun-kissed snowflakes decorated the branches of evergreens like glitter and blanketed the slope leading up to my holiday hideaway, my castle in the clouds, my newfound Christmas star.

But this Christmas there'd be no last-minute shopping frenzy. No Christmas cards or pumpkin pie. No gifts with a name tag reading *Vicki* beneath the family tree. No family at all, for that matter. This year I'd be far from home, like so many others who were here at this Christian conference center. America, Holland, South Africa, Germany, Poland . . . we were a little United Nations gathered in the Austrian Alps. We were college students, many of us studying abroad for a year. Young. Single. Idealistic. In love with Jesus and the hope that one life really could make a difference in the world.

It was a decade before the Berlin wall would come down in Germany. Three decades before the Twin Towers would fall. I'd find the history to come as unbelievable as the history that lay behind me—and beneath me. The castle in which I stood was an SS headquarters during World War II, a "research institute" where 15 women prisoners were held. Before then, the castle had been home to Austrian governors, Bavarian nobles, and feudal lords. Ancient instruments of torture found in the dungeon had long since been transferred to a museum in Salzburg. Since its completion in 1150, Schloss Mittersill had burned to the ground once, been rebuilt, and then set on fire by lightning once more. It had stood fire free for the last 40 years.

During my visit, the only flames I saw there were on the candles that lit the branches of the Christmas tree, except for those painted on the outside wall of the adjacent *gasthaus*. I couldn't walk by the guest house without stopping, staring, or, on occasion, wiping unexpected tears from my wind-burned cheeks. Within a medallion-shaped frame, there was a rendering of the gasthaus on fire. The exact building was depicted right down to the butter-colored exterior and red and white geometric designs on the front door. Towering above the burning building was an Atlas-sized young warrior holding a red banner in one hand while pouring a flask of water to douse the flames in the other. He looked like a painted prayer for help—or thanks.

There were so many people here whose houses were on fire. The student seeking political asylum from Poland. My Jewish roommate who begrudgingly came along because she had nowhere else to go for the holidays. My three new friends from South Africa who would soon return home to escalating racial turmoil. And below us, the town of Mittersill itself. About 5,000 people, yet only one family known to wholeheartedly believe in the true meaning of Christmas. In my mind, the picture-perfect Christmas village was on fire, but they didn't even know it.

On Christmas Eve, our little international group of students dressed in layers of wool, denim, fleece, and whatever else we could get our hands on. We traveled down the winding road to the town below with crumpled songbooks in our hands. The pages were worn from use and stained with hot cocoa and cider, souvenirs of celebrations passed. But it didn't matter. We knew most of the words by heart. All except for our German finale of "Stille Nacht."

The chorus of "O Come, All Ye Faithful," sung with a potluck of accents and mispronounced words, filled the halls of the local hospital with a surprisingly unified sound. As we continued out into the icy slick streets of town, our group of 20 or so became bolder in harmony and volume. We sang as we passed gift shops and bakeries strung with Christmas lights, doors locked tight until the holiday was through. In front of the church, the town cemetery glowed with flickering candles, reminders of those missing from around the tree. We continued into the nearby neighborhoods, making our way through the maze of streets until we reached one small, gabled house.

There we knocked, paused, and then put our whole hearts into our German rendition of "Silent Night." The door opened. Grinning and shivering, the Austrian family inside ventured out to join us in the snow-speckled night air. We lit our candles, one flame spilling over to light the next and the next. We handed the last candle to the man on the doorstep, a stranger to most of us, but no stranger to God. One man in a city of 5,000.

Later that evening, from our eagle's eye view of Mittersill on the castle grounds, we continued our caroling. Huddled around a towering pine that shone softly with the light of dozens of sputtering candles, we joined together to sing "O Little Town of Bethlehem," with one minor revision. We changed "Bethlehem" to "Mittersill." It just seemed to fit. The "hopes and fears of all the years" could still be met in "thee" tonight.

The castle grounds on which we stood had risen from the ashes. It had been the home to depravity, but now held a chorus of praise. For me it became a touchstone, a reminder that one life could make a difference, for better—or for worse. I had a choice. I could set fires or douse them. *Lord, make me a flask of water, flowing freely from Your almighty hands. . . .*

Jesus said, "Rivers of living water will brim and spill
out of the depths of anyone who believes in me."
John 7:38 (*The Message*)

PERSONAL JOURNEY

NAME one person whose life has made a tremendous difference in the world. What do you think made that person's influence so great? In what ways are you alike, and different, from that person?

WHO has God used to be a positive influence in your life? In what specific ways has that person's life changed yours?

WHO is in your "circle of influence"? If you could change your influence on others in any way, what would it be?

READ 2 Corinthians 12:9. List ways God has used your weaknesses in a positive way in the past.

RIGHT now, do you feel more like a flask of water or a house on fire? Spend some time honestly talking to God about where you are spiritually, physically, and emotionally on this leg of your journey—and about how His divine influence can flow more freely through you.

Journey Toward . . .

REMEMBRANCE

Angkor Wat,
Cambodia

F ace-to-face with a lion, it returned my stare with stone-still eyes.

"They found it while filming *Tomb Raider* here last year," our guide said. "People walked right by it for years and never saw it. The jungle hides so much."

Like landmines, as well as lions. Every guidebook I'd read emphasized the importance of staying on the cleared paths, since live explosives were still being uncovered on a regular basis here

As our small group rounded a curve in the trail, the men came into view.

in Cambodia. Wonder, mixed with wariness, tempered my steps as I made my way through a small portion of the vast grounds of Angkor, an ancient religious complex larger than the size of Manhattan.

Lions and temples and landmines, oh my . . . a jumbled jingle danced its way through my mind. But unlike Dorothy, I hadn't entered a land of make-believe. It only felt that way. The Terrace of the Leper King. The bas-relief of *The Churning of the Ocean of Milk*. The Island of the Coiled Serpents. The Citadel of the Cells. The Terrace of Elephants . . . Every stop on the dirt road felt like a potential title for a Stephen King novel.

But my most anticipated destination, the one I'd traveled to in my thoughts for well over 20 years, was Angkor Wat, considered one of the top ten manmade wonders of the world. Its towers, first freed from the encroaching jungle in the late nineteen century, beckoned like a mythical Shangri-la. Water buffalo, banyan trees, and blue sky framed the temple's reflection in the water of the moat surrounding the complex. I hardly noticed the children tugging at my clothing, trying to sell me postcards, as I crossed the causeway that intersected the reflecting pool. Mythical nagas, multiple-headed cobras, rendered in stone formed the balustrades. The closer I got, the more amazing the central structure before me appeared. Terraces, colonnades, towers upon towers, all adorned with a frenzy of almost 2,000 carvings. Overwhelmed by unlimited curiosity wrestling with limited time, I now had to answer the question, "Which way to go first?"

My eyes were drawn to the tower in the center. It loomed like a mammoth cob of shucked corn covered in sandstone, rising more than 200 feet above the ground. The only possible answer to my question was "Up." As I drew closer to the steps clinging to the steep sides of the conical tower, I noticed they were about a foot high, only six inches deep, and crumbling. A Japanese tourist in strappy gold stilettos started sidestepping her way up. Certainly my tennis shoes could do nothing less than accept the gauntlet thrown down before them.

I took my first step up. My guide, Som, cried out in panic, "You're not going up there!"

I hesitated. "Am I not supposed to?"

"Well, you can, but it's dangerous," he said. "You could fall!"

"I promise I won't," I replied, with a decidedly overconfident tone. I glanced up at the woman in heels, inching her way to the top. "I'll be back!" I called over my shoulder and began my ascent.

With a sigh, my guide decided he'd follow the renegade tourist entrusted to his care, leaving the rest of the group to safely wander the galleries of bas-relief below.

When I'd climbed as high as the steps would take me, Som and I followed terraced passageways around in a square. I ran my fingers over the edge of stone etched over 800 years before. *It's not a dream. I'm really here. Angkor Wat, at last.*

Angkor, which means "Holy City," was the capital of the Khmer civilization between the ninth and fifteenth centuries. Over a million people once lived in the area surrounding the temple where I stood. Now, other than the steady flow of tourists and people selling trinkets, the land seemed mostly populated by trees. But spread across the surrounding 77 square miles, 72 temples and stone structures had been freed from the jungle's grip. I wish I could visit them all, explore their nooks and crannies, and let my storyteller's heart tell me tales of what might have been.

"It's beautiful, isn't it?" Som asked. It's the kind of question where the landscape provides its own reply. "But the jungle can take it all back, you know. You'd be surprised how fast. I'll take you to a place where we've let the jungle keep the temple it hid for so many years." He headed back toward the stairs. Som knew just the right words to make me follow.

Inching down the stairs was much more anxiety inducing than traveling up, but I kept my promise and didn't fall. However, when the lens cap came off my camera and clattered down the steps to the courtyard below, Som gave me a look a father would give a child who had one last chance before ending up in the corner.

We returned to the van and drove a few miles, looking like a cloud of red dust out for an afternoon stroll down the bumpy dirt road. When we pulled off into a small car park, I could see nothing but matted vines and the twisted trunks of banyan trees.

"Ta Phrom," Som announced, leading our group of four toward a thin path. The area looked as if it could be totally overgrown and invisible in a matter of days. Our arrival at the temple did not look that much different than our journey toward it. Ta Phrom was more jungle than temple. Powerful banyan trees had toppled moss-covered stones as if they were children's blocks. Cobralike roots had slithered up through doorways and under porticos. In the struggle between man and nature, it appeared nature had won. In an impish tirade, nature had tossed a stone jigsaw puzzle to the floor.

I climbed up and over tiled walkways, through lopsided doorframes, and between tree roots the size of compact cars. I felt like Mary Lennox entering the "secret garden," enchanted by every inch of what she saw. I pulled away from my travel companions, wanting to be alone with the wonder of it all. I didn't want to talk. All I wanted to do was explore, dream, and feel.

As always, time forced me to abandon my ancient playhouse too soon. The van had moved to a different location and we would take a mini jungle trek to rejoin it at yet another temple. The humid afternoon air pushed in close as we twisted our way through the anorexic path. Above the buzz of pesky insects another sound was growing louder as we continued forward. The sound of bamboo flutes and stringed instruments, with quick interludes of conversation and laughter, wafted through the trees.

As our small group rounded a curve in the trail, the men came into view. My first glimpse of the band of musicians spoke louder than any guidebook warning . . . contorted bodies, limbs missing, a dusty jar on the ground nearby labeled *Donations for Landmine Victims*. The men's demeanor was cordial and casual as we passed, while the smile on my face felt forced and unnatural. It was difficult to mask the horror I felt. I knew Cambodia was not a destination to be taken lightly. But it's hard to come face-to-face with what you'd much rather ignore, deny, or hope the jungle will cover so completely that you almost forget it's there. However, Cambodia won't let you forget the past. This is a land of remembrance, a place where yesterdays often shout louder than today.

In a small way, I could relate. For the last five years I'd battled some noisy yesterdays that dragged me through panic attacks and depression. Only recently had I made it back out into the bright sunlight of day. Next to the people of Cambodia, the "landmines" I'd been trying to disarm in my life looked more like firecrackers. But that didn't mean that when they went off in my face they didn't hurt. Years of trying to ignore the past, deny it, or hope the jungle of time would hide it from view so I could forget it completely hadn't worked. Through prayer and wise counsel, God instilled in me the lesson the people of Cambodia had learned so well. Remembrance is a part of healing and wholeness. Not a place to set up camp, but to travel through. Tragedy, as well as triumph, is an integral part of the story God is writing in my life—and in Som's.

"I was 13 years old when everything changed," Som said softly, a dramatic change from his usually vibrant, lighthearted tone. "First the Khmer Rouge killed the soldiers. Then those who were educated. Then the rich. Then anyone they wanted. I was pulled away from my family. They separated us into groups by age. The first lesson we learned is that we could no longer use the word *my*. No more *my father, my mother, my brother . . .*"

"Did anyone in your family die?" asked the man to my left.

Som paused. "Everyone here has lost someone. No family in Cambodia is complete," was his quiet response. "After the war, I was picking fruit on a little hill. A piece of fruit fell off the tree and I bent over to pick it up. Beneath it, I saw bones. It was not a hill. It was a mass grave."

The first such grave had been uncovered in 1980, shortly after the genocide ended. This plot of land became known as the Killing Fields. But it's far from being the only one. Like landmines, mass graves are still being found. Siem Reap, which is the city closest to Angkor, overflows with people, bicycles, rickshaws, upscale hotels, makeshift homes, and roadside markets. But in a bustling patchwork of life our van passed empty squares, desolate vacant lots. The colored flags marking these mass gravesites hung limp in the breathless afternoon air.

Our final stop was the Choeng Ek extermination camp. At first glance it looked like another large empty lot. But more than 17,000 people died on the land where I stood. In contrast to the ancient columns of stacked stones we'd wandered through all morning, a single column rose before us now. It was a tall Plexiglas pillar sandwiched between a plaster base and cap—filled with bones. Skulls with vacant eye sockets mingled with bones from arms and legs. Legs that once ran and danced. Arms that held loved ones and worked in the fields. Eyes whose final glimpse of this earth had been one of horror.

For a moment, not one of us spoke. It felt irreverent to try to express something for which there are no words. I wanted to turn away, to look back toward the jungle where I could lose myself in the mystery of the distant past. The artifacts left by the people of Angkor testified to how they lived, while the artifacts of the recent past couldn't help but cry out how these people died.

Out of the 7.3 million people who lived in Cambodia in 1975, between 1.5 and 2 million disappeared by 1979. These bones, as well as those of so many others, continue to serve as a memorial to those who died. But they also provide concrete evidence of evil. They're reminders of atrocities that dumbfound the mind, souvenirs of journeys no human heart should ever have to take. They give witness to a story that these individuals are no longer able to tell. A story of resistance, resilience, and power gone wrong. A story I can learn from. A story that has now become part of my own.

> *You'll use the old rubble of past lives to build anew, rebuild the foundations from out of your past. You'll be known as those who can fix anything, restore old ruins, rebuild and renovate, make the community livable again.*
> Isaiah 58:12 (*The Message*)

PERSONAL JOURNEY

WHERE did this journey to Cambodia take you spiritually and emotionally? What did God say to you along the way?

THINK of the top news stories in the world today. Do you find it hard to understand human suffering in light of an all-powerful, all-loving God? What part does free will play in it all?

MAKE a list of the top three experiences you'd like to remember—and forget. How can God use all of these to help you rebuild, restore, and renovate your own life? What's the difference between remembrance and reliving something in your mind over and over again?

TO disarm a landmine, first it has to be uncovered. Are there any personal landmines you can think of that need to be brought out into the open?

PRAYERFULLY read Isaiah 61:1–4 (NIV). God calls you an "oak of righteousness, a planting of the LORD for the display of his splendor." What does that mean to you? Ask Him how He can use you to rebuild that which may have been in ruins for generations.

Assisi,
Italy

The church seemed conflicted. Maybe even a little bipolar. Large and lumpy, it dominated the crest of the grass green slope, as well as much of the town of Assisi. The angular bell tower stuck out from the curved cupolas and colonnade like an awkward adolescent boy who'd undergone a sudden growth spurt. Guess that's what happens when you try to roll two churches into one. The Italians referred to the upper and lower

I'd fooled myself that day in Assisi as thoroughly as I'd fooled the women behind the counter.

basilicas as *superiore* and *inferiore*. I didn't need a translator to help me determine which basilica I'd rather be.

One high, one low. One light, one dark. One superiore, one inferiore. A little bit Gothic, a little bit Romanesque. Two distinct chapels combined to make one church. From the hilltop vista where I sat, the outcome looked like an uneasy partnership. But I figured the basilica's namesake could probably relate. For the man who would be known as Saint Francis, dichotomy began at birth. His mother wanted to name him Giovanni. His father pushed for Francesco. The will of his wealthy father won out. The Bernardones named their Italian-born baby "Little Frenchman."

When the ruling parties of the Guelphs and the Ghibellines fought for control of Assisi, Francesco was taken prisoner. That's when Francesco's teenage dreams of military glory began to shift toward glorifying God. Soon Francesco chose to trade privilege for poverty. Instead of hobnobbing with the rich and famous, he tended lepers. He started a religious order based on chastity, poverty, and obedience, tenets about as popular back then as they would be today. The once-arrogant young man became known for his humility, selflessness, and tenderness toward all of God's creatures.

Giovanni, Francesco. Guelph, Ghibelline. Wealth, poverty. Pride, humility. Self-centered, God-centered . . . Francesco of Assisi was a human tug-of-war. And the first real signs of a battle began in his late teens and early 20s. Guess I wasn't so odd after all. Here I sat on a hillside in Assisi, an American college student studying in Italy, feeling pulled in opposing directions. Who was I? Who did God create me to be? And where was I supposed to go from here?

Even my trip to Assisi began with conflict. Trains came and went . . . 5:00 A.M. . . . 5:15 . . . 5:30 . . . and still I sat. I was supposed to be on my way to Rome with a couple of friends. Friends who never showed. Did they oversleep or have second thoughts? My annoyance waged war with my self-confidence. But I was still faced with a decision. I had one more month in Italy before returning home to the US after ten months abroad. Here I was at a train station with money for a ticket in my hand. Numbers and letters flipped on the wall in front of me, listing the trains ready to depart. "Assisi, 5:45." I'd spent an afternoon there once and always wanted to return. Here was my chance.

After settling into my train compartment, I realized I had a rare opportunity. Today, I could travel incognito. Without a group of English-speaking friends surrounding me, maybe I could blend in. Act as though I belonged. Feign I was *Italiana* instead of *Americana*.

I assessed my disguise. Heavy Italian eye makeup? Check. Dress and comfortable heels instead of jeans and tennis shoes? Check. Hair permed as tightly as a Renaissance Shirley Temple? Check. Italian book to read on the train? Check. (As long as fellow passengers didn't notice that I read about one page every five minutes—and if I kept my handy Italian dictionary hidden in my purse.) My self-assigned mission was a "go."

The train ride was easy. I kept my nose buried in my book or my eyes focused on a distant horizon through the train window. Upon my arrival, catching the bus up the hill from the train station only required a one-word inquiry, "Assisi?" At that moment I was glad I hadn't ventured to Civita di Bagnoregio or some other mouthful-of-syllables destination. The cordial bus driver assured me I was headed in the right direction.

When I finally arrived in Saint Francis's hometown, I remembered why my first visit had left me wanting more. The warm tone of the stone buildings was unlike so many other Italian towns I'd visited. Instead of the usual goldenrod-colored masonry, the walls were the soft pink and white of a baby carnation. Window boxes, flowerpots, and urns overflowed with blossoms in gemstone hues. Embroidered shirts, dresses, bags, tablecloths, shawls, wall hangings, you name it, filled gift shop windows and spilled out into the main square, enticing visitors to finger the delicate handiwork that was the region's specialty. I tried to silence the shopper within who madly pointed out patterns and florals that could fill the last few open spaces in my luggage. One last splurge before I returned home to the land of look-alike malls.

Maybe on my way back down I'll browse a while, I consoled myself. I continued my trek along almost deserted, flower-lined lanes. Even my Italian heels wouldn't prevent me from reaching my final destination. As always, I would travel up. Up to the top of the hill. Up to Saint Francis's cathedral and beyond. Up to La Rocca, the medieval fortress that towered above the town.

Assisi seemed unusually quiet, almost deserted, prepared to offer me a respite from the noise and crowds of my temporary home in Florence. After a bit of rest and reverie on the slope above the Basilica di San Francesco, I continued climbing toward the castle that dominated the hill. Although a chill still hung in the air, just a hint of a warm spring breeze played with my newly permed curls. I took off my coat and slung it over my arm. It had been a long winter. Damp. Rainy. Sullen gray. Just seeing the sun set high in a cloudless sky seemed to renew my energy, and my hope.

A bit winded, but buoyed with the joy of accomplishment, I reached the outer walls of La Rocca. Now for the payoff. I turned around.

Below me, a sea of verdant hills, rounded and rolling. Scattered patches of freshly turned earth, vineyards, and fields eager for spring. Through it all a white ribbon of road unfurled, partially lined with pencil-thin cypress trees. I kicked off my heels and plopped myself down in the newborn spring grass. If ever there was a place to think, to pray, to get things in perspective, this had to be it. Maybe that's why Saint Francis ultimately stuck around his hometown. He had a traveler's heart like mine and journeyed to places like Egypt, Spain, and Israel. But he always came home. He died right here in Assisi, the same place where he'd been born.

But I didn't want to go home. Today, anyway. Tomorrow I could swing back to wanting to catch the next plane to the States. But after so many months of being a *straniera* (a foreigner) I was finally beginning to fit in. I'd grown comfortable with using the name "Vittoria" because "Vicki" was judged too short and childish by my Italian friends. I knew how to ask the butcher at the market to "please, cut the feet off my chicken." I could calculate the conversion of thousands of lire into the equivalent of a few measly dollars in my head. I knew how to push, shove, and shout to get waited on, because in Italy patience is considered a waste of time, not a virtue, and forming a line is merely an exercise in futility.

In Italy I enjoyed new friends, new food, new vistas, and a new freedom. Sure, I missed Mexican food, reliable utilities, and relational bonds that had been forged over the years. Maybe the real truth was I didn't want to choose. I wanted the familiarity of the old life and the excitement of the new.

Well, what I really wanted was to get married, have kids, travel, and write. But that was a pretty unlikely scenario. I could count the number of dates I'd had through high school and college on my fingers. My grandmother always said if I just lost a little weight, I could get a man. Well, instead of taking her advice, I rented an apartment above a bakery when I moved to Italy—and put on 40 pounds in ten months. That's what happens when before sunrise every morning the aroma of *biscotti* and *panettone* fill your dreams. Soon you find your pantry is filled with whatever the *pasticceria* happens to have on sale. In my 20-year-old mind, being shy and overweight (not to mention having an Italian perm that would resemble a strawberry blonde scouring pad for months to come) was the kiss of death for potential married bliss.

As for becoming a writer, I was determined to finish my degree in journalism. Afterward, I'd probably resort to what my parents always believed to be my backup plan. I'd become a secretary. And not many secretaries I knew took vacations in Italy to casually linger over Tuscan vistas.

Vicki, Vittoria. American, Italian. Chunky, svelte. Single, married. Writer, secretary . . . Conflicted, you bet. That's when the pity party truly began. Right there on the grounds of La Rocca. It felt as though God gave me dreams too big for my life to hold. So like Jonah, I decided to run in the opposite direction. I made up a new life plan. One that looked godly on the outside. After graduation, I would head to a kibbutz in Israel. I would learn Greek and Hebrew, so I could read the Bible in the original language and get a better handle on what God was saying to me. I would bury myself in my studies, continue to learn new languages, and involve myself in some kind of humanitarian work. In some remote, exotic locale, of course. Like Saint Francis, I'd give up everything for God. . . .

The putt-putt of a sputtering motorbike pulled me back from dreams of the future to the present. A monk buzzed by on a Vespa, his black robes flapping in the wind like an earthbound crow. I rose, dusting stray blades of grass from my skirt. Surveying the landscape below, I felt a renewed sense of purpose. I was simply a vessel in God's hands. A piece of clay. What I wanted didn't matter. It was up to the Potter to shape my future.

I strode back down the hill, my head held high. I grabbed a quick panini for lunch, visited a few landmarks, and rechecked the schedule for my return trip. While waiting for the bus, I decided to visit one of the gift shops I'd ogled on the way up.

Two women chatted behind the counter at the back of the store. I smiled in their direction and echoed back their warm *"Buon giorno!"* Both wore the uniform of small-town Italian matrons: a shapeless black dress; pewter hair pulled back tightly in a bun; support hose as thick as sweat socks; and drab, sensible shoes. I liked them immediately. Their animated chatter continued as I walked through the souvenir-cluttered aisles, drawn to piles of brightly embroidered shirts. As I wandered, I listened.

What began as simply practicing my Italian soon turned into eavesdropping. They were talking about me. They were arguing over where I was from.

"France?"

"*Boh!* She's Italian!"

"I don't know, maybe she's German!"

"*Boh!* Italian, I say!"

"But look at her hair!" They both paused and stared. Red hair wasn't all that common in Italy, unless it was dyed almost burgundy; but along the northern border seeing a redheaded Italian wasn't totally out of the question.

The exchange went back and forth a few more times. But one nationality they never mentioned was American. When I brought my delicately embroidered dress up to the counter, one woman asked, "*Italiana?*"

"*No, Americana,*" I responded.

They responded with a chorus of surprised *bohs*, which I took it as a compliment. I thanked them for my purchase and waved a quick "*Ciao!*"

Mission accomplished. I'd pulled off my transformation. I was no longer *Americana*, but *Italiana!*

Of course, I really wasn't. I remained as American as the day I had moved to Florence. Sure, I'd picked up a bit of the language, adapted to a few customs, and changed my hair. But that didn't change who I was. That had not changed who God created me to be.

I'd fooled myself that day in Assisi just as thoroughly as I'd fooled the women behind the counter. Wanting to move to a kibbutz was all about hiding from God, not honoring Him. If I buried what my heart really longed for, then when my dreams didn't materialize, God wouldn't look bad, right? And maybe I wouldn't ache from a broken heart.

That day my God was so small; He could have fit into those spaces I left in my luggage. But He didn't stay that way. Day after day, year after year, He continues to burst out of every box I try to put Him in. I wouldn't expect anything less from a living, loving, almighty God. Of course, I continue to burst out of the box I try and fit myself into as well. That's because it's this same approachable, yet unfathomable, God who shaped my heart, as well as my physical frame. He's the author of my deepest, truest, most honest dreams. And more often than not, I find it's my own plans that are too small.

I never moved to Israel and lived on a kibbutz. I never learned to read Greek and Hebrew. I never worked with a humanitarian effort overseas. At least, not yet. Instead, I returned to the US from Italy, after gaining yet a few more pounds. My first week back at college, I met a fellow student named Mark who fell in love with me—all of me. We picked out our future son's name on our first date. For the next 25 years, my husband and I raised two great kids, while I wrote in my spare time. And every so often, a wild opportunity would come up for me to travel to some exotic locale, like Thailand, Peru, or China. I can't wait to see what God has planned for me next. It may set me dancing. It may break my heart. It may pull me in a different direction than I ever thought I'd go. All I know is like Francesco, the closer I draw to God, the more my true identity will be revealed.

> *God rewrote the text of my life when I opened the*
> *book of my heart to his eyes.*
> Psalm 18:24 (*The Message*)

PERSONAL JOURNEY

HOW has God "rewritten the text of your life"? Have any of your dreams changed as you've gotten to know God better?

RECALL a time when you felt like a foreigner or an outsider. Did you do anything special to try to fit in? Do you think Jesus ever felt like an "outsider" here on earth?

IS there any area where you currently feel conflicted, like you're being torn in opposing directions? Consider the words of Matthew 10:39. Is there something you need to "lose"?

DO you know your true identity? Take a quick trip through Ephesians, reading verses 1:4–5; 2:10; 2:19; 4:22–24; and 5:15–17. Write a brief paragraph describing God's unique creation of you.

HOW does recognizing who God created you to be help you better understand God's purpose for your life?

Santa Fe,
New Mexico

H er . . . I want her," I said, pointing to the woman basking in the Santa Fe sunshine. Barefoot, eyes closed, head tilted back ever so slightly, she seemed to be sending silent praise toward the skies. Her robust curves and burnished black skin glistened in the afternoon light. She'd sit by my front door, welcoming friends and strangers alike to come in and stay a while.

Come as you are, she'd whisper. *Breathe deep. Beauty lingers here.*

I pictured the artists at work over their masterpieces, expressing something too deep for words.

I ran my finger along the curve of her shoulder. It was hard to believe she was only bronze. I flipped over the price tag.

"I think she's decided to stay right here," I told my friend Pam. "She costs as much as my car."

The woman relaxing in the sun was my all-around winner. Pam's was a loosely woven textile, knotted threads of fuchsia, plum, crimson, and cobalt. Bright and bold, yet as delicately ethereal as a passing thought, the sculpture was entitled *Prayer III*. Somehow, it fit.

All day long my friend Pam and I wandered the galleries of Canyon Road playing "the game." The rules were simple. Answer two questions: "If money were no object, which piece of art would you take with you?" and "Which piece of art couldn't the gallery pay you to put in your home?"

Pam adored the work of Georgia O'Keeffe, an artist I'd always summed up as "big flowers and cow skulls." I preferred painter Daniel Merriam's whimsical fantasies. Pam responded to wildflower purples, sky blues, and bold, clean lines. I preferred warm Tuscan yellows, whispers of greens, and no clearly defined lines at all. Pam delighted in textiles, woven baskets, and realism. I was pulled toward pottery, mixed mediums, and impressionism. Pam praised a painting's flawless finish. I delighted in brushstrokes of paint slathered on so thick they created shadows. Finding something that resonated deeply with both of us wasn't easy. Then, we walked through the door of the Awakening Museum.

An explosion of praise made visible. A rush of joy too profound for words. A kaleidoscope of color, texture, light, and shadow . . . we'd entered the beating heart of a painted prayer. A vivid collage of images filled every square inch from the back of the door, around the four walls, spilling up and across the vaulted ceiling above, almost 8,000 square feet of artwork in all. Stylized renditions of the Last Supper, the Resurrection, and the glories of heaven were interwoven into a synthesis of story, worship, and wonder.

For over 13 years, artist Jean-Claude Gaugy carved and painted 400 individual wooden panels as an expression of his love for God.

Gaugy didn't begin with an overall plan or preliminary sketch. He simply prayed for direction each day and then went to work. I was awestruck by the seamless complexity of his finished masterpiece, not to mention the depth of his devotion. I could hardly pray for five minutes without getting distracted. I wondered if a true prodigy like Gaugy ever doubted his talent. If he had days where he was frustrated, where the lines didn't flow, and the inspiration didn't come. I wondered if he was anything at all like me.

I reclined on one of the couches in the middle of the room so I could take in the enormity of the jagged bursts of light depicting heaven above me. It was one artist's take on the original Artist Himself. The mediums God used were far superior to any we'd seen used today in Santa Fe. Instead of wood and paint, canvas and clay, God's almighty hands wielded time, space, energy, matter, light, and life itself. But in some ways the end result was the same. God created monumental works of art. But then the Artist did something without precedent. His gave His masterpieces free will.

Imagine, an Artist inviting His creation to work hand-in-hand with Him to complete itself. But that's just what God did. As living, breathing, freewilled works of art, God's masterpieces can choose to draw near to their Creator or push Him away. They can choose good or evil, blessings or curses, life or death. And the choices they make change the form that they take.

I wondered what the masterpiece of "me" looked like in God's eyes. *How does who I am today compare with the finished work of art I'll become? And what's the best way to get to there from here?*

My heart knew the answer in an instant. Who knows better how to complete a masterpiece than the Master who envisioned it? Like a child who learns to dance by standing on her father's shoes, I longed to put my hands on God's and follow His lead as He swept life's paintbrush of color, shadow, and perspective into my life. I smiled to myself. *And, Lord, don't forget to put that paint on good and thick. . . .*

Walking out of the museum felt like exiting a powerful church service on Sunday morning. Outside, a quote from Pablo Picasso graced a niche of flowered trellises: "Art washes away from the soul the dust of everyday life." So true. Today's sermon had been carved in wood and voiced in paint. With inspired eloquence it spoke without saying a word.

Pam and I continued our journey through the galleries near the main square, effusively praising any particular artist or piece that "spoke" to us. To me every piece of art looked like a miniature miracle. I pictured the artists at work over their masterpieces, expressing something too deep for words. Something too big to hold inside. Something they could only communicate through the work of their hands.

After listening to my friend and me excitedly ooze adjectives for several minutes, one gallery owner asked, "Are you artists?"

Pam and I laughed, then hemmed and hawed. We looked at each other rather sheepishly and replied, "No, we just like to look."

"But what about those quilts you make?" I whispered to Pam after the woman had turned away. "And your scrapbooking and handmade jewelry and cards? You said you painted with watercolors . . ."

"Well, what about you," she retorted. "What about your writing and all those photos you take? What about your music?"

We were artists. Inside we both knew it was true. After all, hadn't we planned this whole weekend together to "feed our artist's heart"? Why was it so hard to admit that we followed in our Father's artistic footsteps? Why should we be surprised that being created in the likeness of the ultimate Artist, we felt a need to create?

It seemed all of Santa Fe felt that pull. From the architecture to the couture to the cuisine, there was so much more "art" here than what was on display in the galleries. And above the chic shops, winding lanes, and adobe courtyards, God exhibited His artistic display. Aspen trees dressed in fall colors swathed the surrounding hills in a soft palette of gold and green. My favorite. The first response from my artist's heart was praise. It was only later I would feel the pull to paint the beauty in words.

> *We are God's masterpiece. He has created us anew*
> *in Christ Jesus, so that we can do the good things*
> *he planned for us long ago.*
> Ephesians 2:10 (NLT)

PERSONAL JOURNEY

WHAT kind of art do you like best? What do you think this says about the way God designed you?

IN the original Greek, the word "masterpiece" in Ephesians 2:10 is *poiema*, the word from which *poem* is derived. How does it feel to view yourself as a poem or masterpiece? What part does "good works" play in completing the piece of art entitled *You*?

READ Exodus 28:2–5 and 35:30 to 36:5; Psalm 45:1 and 96:1. What value does God place on creativity? Remember, what's important to God should be important to you.

SINCE God is the ultimate Artist and you're created in His image, there's an artist hidden in you. Are you familiar with that aspect of yourself? Talk to God about how He's wired you to express your creativity. It may be through music, cooking, dance, carpentry, scrapbooking, hospitality, writing, photography, home decorating, sculpting, gardening . . . who knows? Then, journal what God teaches you about Himself and your own heart in the process.

HOW do you use your creativity to honor God? Use your own unique art form to worship God in a brand-new way.

Skagway,
Alaska

E ither that's really easy or she's really good!" commented the first-timer standing next to me.

"She's really good," I answered back. I squinted skyward, cocking my neck at an uncomfortably steep angle to get a better look. My 18-year-old daughter scaled the 60-foot rock wall like a lizard scampering up a backyard fence. Katrina was in her element, doing what she loved. And she wanted to share it with me. That's why

"Now all you have to do is lean backward over the edge . . ."

my stomach felt like one of the pebbles knocked loose during my daughter's ascent, tumbling out of control toward solid ground. I'd promised I'd go next.

In principle, rock climbing always sounded like fun. I enjoy the outdoors. I like hiking. I love climbing countless stairs to the tip-top of steeples, towers, and windblown vistas to get the ultimate overview of what lies below. But today, standing at the bottom of a cliff strapped into what felt like a trapeze artist's chastity belt, I felt that perhaps my enthusiasm had been premature. Perhaps I preferred rock climbing as more of a spectator sport.

But I'd made a promise.

"On belay," I said to the mountain guide who was holding the rope that was holding me. That was climbing talk for "ready." Which, of course, I was not.

"Belay is on," she replied. Such a tiny young woman holding my life in her hands. I hoped she lifted weights in her spare time.

I took one quick nervous glance up the wall. The structure wasn't as dramatically vertical or as tall as the portion Katrina had so casually ambled her way up. Only the height of, say, a four-story building. Too bad a Spider-Man suit wasn't included with the white helmet and nifty, leather climbing shoes.

I'd been assured, and reassured, I couldn't fall. The guide's firm hold on the rope that secured my harness would hold me steady if I slipped or lost my grip. Again, in principle, that sounded fine. Then why were my hands starting to sweat? It certainly wasn't the heat. It was in the 50s and overcast, typical for an Alaskan spring day. I wiped my hands on my pants, took a deep breath, and reached heavenward. I wrapped my fingers around a tiny rock jutting out from above my head, balanced one foot on a small ledge and pushed myself up. So far, so good. Six inches off the ground.

Unlike my daughter's playful lizard approach to rock climbing, my style resembled that of an inebriated snail. I stretched and strained and lurched and grasped and slipped and slithered up the wall. But I didn't fall. Thanks to a trustworthy belayer. But long before I reached the top I knew my rock climbing debut would also be my farewell tour. I'd keep my promise and complete the climb. But my next three "turns" would be donated to other participants who actually enjoyed the process of having their arms pulled out of their sockets while balancing precariously on one big toe and Eskimo-kissing slimy dew-coated rocks with their nose.

Once I made it to the top, I was so relieved that my muscles, twitching from exhaustion, would soon be able to rest, that I forget to take a quick look around before I began my descent. At that moment, all I wanted to see was solid ground beneath my own two feet. I bounced my way down, pushing myself away from the rock and then trying to stop myself from slamming back full force into it. My technique wasn't pretty, but it got me back where I belonged.

Once on the ground, I realized my mistake. I'd gone through all that hard work, taken what felt like a tremendous risk, and forgotten to do the one thing I was really looking forward to doing, taking in the view. Now I was back beneath a thick ceiling of pines. That's OK. I'll buy a postcard, I reassured my weary self.

My daughter hurried over to the boulder I'd seated myself on.

"So, what'd ya think?" she said. "Did you love it?"

I looked up at Katrina with what felt like very old, very out-of-shape eyes. "Can't say I did," I answered back. "I think I'm going to call it a day."

I could read the disappointment on Katrina's face. I understood. I know what it's like to love something and want someone you care about to understand, and share, that same rush you feel. But if I could live with her not appreciating raspberry jalapeño hot fudge on ice cream like I did, she could live with me not swooning over the thrill of rock climbing.

"But you're still going to rappel, right?" Katrina asked tentatively.

"Huh?" was all that my fear-stricken brain could come up with.

"It's really fun and not as hard as climbing. You just walk

backward down the wall . . ." She was pointing to the Empire State Building-sized rock face she'd mastered earlier.

I felt my stomach hit the floor once more. Then I looked at my daughter's eager expression. I didn't have to go. I was the oldest member of the group, old enough to be well past the stage of feeling I had to prove myself to anyone. Even to my own sweet daughter. But I trusted her. She wouldn't lead me anywhere she didn't think I was up to going. True, she—OK, and myself as well—had overestimated my level of fitness and underestimated my threshold of terror when it came to hauling myself up the side of a cliff. But down? That could be a whole different story. This time gravity would be on my side. Besides, it would give me a chance to take in the view I'd missed the first time around.

"OK." Too small syllables. One big commitment.

But for the next hour I could relax. Well, as much as a soft, squishy person can relax while sitting on a hard, pointy boulder. I watched the rest of the group trying their hand at progressively more difficult climbs. My husband was struggling to master a tricky overhang Katrina had just completed. (Yes, my husband, Mark, was there too. I just chose not to mention him earlier because, although he was a novice like me, he seemed to have been the original carrier of the "lizard" gene my daughter inherited. In other words, when it came to rock climbing, he was a natural. But at this moment, he happened to be struggling, which makes it a less personally humiliating time for me to bring him into the story.) After several gallant tries, Mark resorted to an alternate route. But he still made it to the top in what—at least from my lowly perch—seemed like record time.

Time continued passing, as it tends to do. All too soon the time came for our group to hike up to the top of the cliff so we could experience the "joy" of rappelling. The trail was steep and uneven. If only I had on my sturdy hiking boots instead of these balletlike climbing shoes. Tree roots, loose stones, and a slippery layer of dead pine needles formed a natural obstacle course. But the worst was yet to come. My much-anticipated "view" was what nearly did me in.

As we came around the last turn and out onto the plateau that marked the uppermost edge of the cliff, the panorama was dynamic. The dark clouds that hid the sun gave the vista a film noir feel. Shades of white, black, and gray dominated the scene. Jagged slate-colored mountains wrapped in bands of dove gray snow were dotted with what looked like velvet paint-by-number pine trees. I could hear the rush of the Yukon River at the bottom of the gorge far below, even though it was hidden from sight.

On the opposite side of the ravine, I traced the clean-cut path of railroad tracks up the side of the mountain. On our drive up to our climb, we'd seen the White Pass Railway chugging up those tracks. As early as 1898, that same railway began transporting fortune-seekers during the Klondike gold rush. Today, its 1890s-style cars transport more than 250,000 passengers each year on a 20-mile climb up the pass. Instead of gold, tourists now come searching for the perfect photograph. They hang over railings in between cars, trying to capture on film how precariously the tracks seem to cling to the side of a sheer granite wall. I knew how those cars felt.

If only I'd kept my eyes on the railroad tracks. Unfortunately, I walked to the edge of the cliff and took a look down. Big mistake. The surge of adrenaline—brought on by sheer terror—raced through my body with such force I thought I was going to fall to my knees. But the thought of falling in any direction at this point seemed like a really bad idea.

I'd never been afraid of heights before. Of course, I'd never before planned to step off the side of a skyscraper either. For a moment, I couldn't speak. And for those who know me personally, they'll attest to the fact that's quite an anomaly. But through a fog of dread I could still hear my daughter's voice. She was volunteering we'd go next.

Not only was I expected to nonchalantly step backward off a skyscraper but I had to do it in front of an audience. I kept repeating to myself, "You don't have to prove anything to anyone. You don't have to prove anything to anyone. You don't have to prove anything to anyone. . . . In a moment you'll be dead and with Jesus, so it'll all be a moot point anyway."

The guides tested the ropes that wound from the metal loop on the edge of the cliff down to the undoubtedly very hard ground below. Like a doll without a will of my own, I allowed the guides to fasten my harness and show me how to let a little rope out at a time to control the speed of my descent.

"Now all you have to do is lean backward over the edge . . ."

Supposedly, this is the moment when your life flashes before your eyes. Instead, my favorite painting flashed through mine: An angel, a pudgy, childlike cherub clinging to a finial at the top of steeple. Above, storm clouds are gathering. Below, trees are bent over from the force of the wind. Shingles on rooftops are unhinged and threatening to fall. Windows have been blown out of the surrounding buildings. Gusts from the impending storm have even loosened a few feathers from the angel's wings. The feathers have taken flight, while the cherub remains earthbound and motionless. With eyes tightly closed, fingers, arms, and even toes are "Holding on Till the End," as the artist so aptly entitled his work.

I fell under the spell of this painting because it reminded me so much of myself. Frightened so much of the time. Not wanting to risk opening my eyes. Tightly clutching the unstable tower of my own abilities and limited understanding. All the while God's softly whispering, *Go ahead and let go. Underneath are My everlasting arms.*

Did I trust that the well-trained guides had secured the ropes that held me? Yes. Did I trust that my daughter desired my best? Yes. Would I put that trust to the test by literally putting my life in someone else's hands? An artist's rendition of what a pair of "everlasting arms" might look like appeared in my mind's eye. My life was already in Someone else's hands.

"Just lean back," the guide gently repeated.

I did.

Like a game of "trust" at a teenage slumber party, I let myself fall backward toward unseen arms. I'd be lying if I didn't admit that my stomach did a swan dive, but it was short lived. The rope harness held fast. Now, all I had to do was change my perspective. My solid ground simply shifted at a 90-degree angle. As I walked backward down the vertical ledge, with my daughter by my side, I started— dare I say it—to actually have fun. As Katrina offered a continual stream of encouragement, I leaned back and enjoyed the scenery, the company, and the satisfaction of having successfully faced my fears. Well, almost successfully. I became a little overconfident in my speedy descent and hit the ground fanny first, instead of feet first. Not so graceful. But definitely grateful. Thankful I'd risked what felt like stepping out on thin air. Thankful I could confidently lean on what I believed would hold. Thankful I could experience the freedom of letting go.

> *The eternal God is your refuge, and underneath*
> *are the everlasting arms.*
> Deuteronomy 33:27 (NIV)

PERSONAL JOURNEY

HAVE you ever tried to do something you were afraid of? What did you learn through the experience?

WHAT is one thing you fear? How do you try to keep yourself safe from this "one thing" in your day-to-day life? What does your fear say about your trust in God?

READ Proverbs 3:5–6. In what ways do you find yourself leaning on your own understanding instead of trusting in God?

PSALM 37:3 (NIV) says, "Trust in the LORD and do good." What part does trust play in enabling you to "do good"?

PAINT your own picture of *Holding on Till the End* in your mind. Is there anything you're holding on to that's preventing you from fully putting your trust in God? Spend some time in prayer talking to God about this area of your life.

Casablanca,

Morocco

A n untimely dusk. The air cools as daylight fades. But the sun still hangs high in the sky. It's only a shadow, you remind yourself. Not the hungry dragon the ancient Chinese believed it to be. Not a judgment from God. Not the end of the world. Just the moon cutting into the dance between the earth and the sun. But in a matter of moments, all you've come to accept about how day and night works is turned on its

*One small bite
of night overtook
the edge of my heart.
The dragon
had risen.*

head. One small bite of night has overtaken the edge of the sun.

During totality you come to understand why the word *eclipse* was derived from the Greek word for abandonment. The ever-reliable sun seems to forsake the earth below. But even then there remains a thin circle of light, a silver promise ring placed on the finger of night. The world holds its breath, waiting for the return of order, hoping things will go back to the way they were before. Maybe a sun-eating dragon doesn't seem that far-fetched.

The hope of standing in the shadow of that dragon leads otherwise rational people to travel thousands of miles. In the early 1970s, that dragon drew my parents and me to the coast of Africa. My scientifically minded father was asked to speak on a cruise ship about the wonders of an impending solar eclipse. Further business would lead him on to Cairo, Paris, Munich, and London.

"I'll do anything to go with you. Anything. . . ." Little did I know those words would haunt me for years to come.

I was 16, naïve, and awkwardly shy. Unaware of cultural mores and foreign customs. Drawn to distant shores by the promise of being close enough to touch what I'd only visited in books . . . the Pyramids, the Eiffel Tower, Stonehenge. But our journey would begin in Morocco. From here our ship would sail into the Atlantic Ocean to intersect with the path of the eclipse.

My first look at the world beyond North American shores was through seriously jet-lagged eyes. But I couldn't turn away. It was like reading the first page of a much-anticipated novel. I had to read on, regardless of how tired I felt.

Casablanca was a frenzied jumble. Block after block of boxy, whitewashed buildings lined a tangle of boulevards and alleyways. Motorbikes darted in and out of traffic. Car horns blared. The pointed hoods of men robed in *djellabas* stood out like exclamation points on the crowded streets. Tidy piles of fresh produce languished in the midday heat. Beneath dusty awnings, vendors hawked their wares, their guttural cries sounding like random letters thrown in a blender. Carved wooden screens filled arched windows, allowing those inside to see out more easily than outsiders could see in. To a not-so-well-traveled teen, the city felt like a place of adventure and intrigue, a mystery novel that promised to hold more than first meets the eye.

But what I remember most about that day is hands. Strangers' hands. For years I was certain there'd been four or five teenagers. There just seemed to be so many hands. But in reality there were only two young boys. Not even men. Still, I couldn't escape.

My parents and I were walking back to the hotel after a late dinner when the boys ran up behind me and reached under my dress. They began kissing me. Fondling me. Tugging at my clothes with eager fingers. Everything seemed to shift into slow motion. I was twisting, pushing, trying to slip away. Fear mixed with shame reduced my cries for help to soft whispers. But above my own almost unrecognizable voice, I heard a sound that felt as foreign as my surroundings. Laughter.

My father's hearty laugh even caught the boys' attention. He asked them to pose for a photo, their hands still draped across my chest. Then with a warm smile, my father presented each of the boys with a handful of coins and a word of thanks. One small bite of night overtook the edge of my heart. The dragon had risen.

I left. I turned my back on my parents and hurried through the dark streets toward the hotel. Betrayal. Fear. Humiliation. Abandonment. Everything spilled over into anger. Hot, molten words ran through my mind, fueling my legs into almost a run. When I reached the hotel room, I turned the dead bolt, locking my parents outside. I only had a moment to pace the room alone, mind racing, anger seething, shame burning. My father began pounding on the door with obvious impatience.

"You always make such a big deal out of nothing!" he called through the door. "Get over it."

Beaten. Exhausted. I slowly turned the latch. I let my parents into the room. But locked my father out of my heart.

Over the next few weeks, I explored the tunnels of the Great

Pyramid, climbed to the top of the Eiffel Tower, stood in the shadow of the monoliths at Stonehenge—and was molested again in Cairo and on the cruise ship. Shamed into silence, I felt I now understood the price I had to pay to see the world. All it cost was a bit of my soul.

But God had other plans. Two years later I allowed the first rays of God's light to penetrate the darkness that covered my life. But when I was faced with God's mandate to forgive others, all I could hear was the hollow echo of my father's words, "You always make such a big deal out of nothing! Get over it." Now my heavenly Father was telling me to do the very same thing. I couldn't. I wouldn't. Surely this was more than God had a right to ask. I worked even harder to keep parts of my heart locked up as best as I could.

But God is a Father who never fails. Who never gives up. Who never abandons those He loves. Thanks to Him, no eclipse lasts forever. Yet for me the dragon's shadow lingered long after totality should have ended. It lasted until I was so tired of darkness that I came to God's door, beaten and exhausted, unlocked the latch on my side and let forgiveness slip in. It had nothing to do with making light of what happened, minimizing the pain, or shifting the blame. But it did mean letting go of bitterness, anger, and the habit of replaying those old travel tapes again and again. It meant opening my heart to love a father who's flawed. Who's made mistakes. Who needs forgiveness. Who needs God. Just like me.

The LORD turns my darkness into light.
2 Samuel 22:29 (NIV)

PERSONAL JOURNEY

HAS there been a total eclipse in your life, something you felt as though you couldn't forgive? If so, what kind of journey has it taken you on? What role has God played in that journey?

EXTENDING forgiveness doesn't mean your emotional heartache immediately disappears. How do you know when you've honestly forgiven someone who has hurt you?

COLOSSIANS 3:13 (NIV) says, "Forgive as the Lord forgave you." Why do you think God takes forgiveness as seriously as He does? How does forgiveness benefit you, as well as the one you're forgiving?

PLANT Ephesians 6:12 (NIV) firmly in your mind. The next time you find yourself struggling to forgive someone, remind yourself that your "struggle is not against flesh and blood." How does this perspective change how you feel about the situation? How does it change how you pray?

CALL to mind a few offenses for which the Lord has forgiven you. Then read Psalm 103:8–12. Rewrite these verses in your own words, a thank-You note to God for who He is and what He's done.

Oahu,

Hawaii

There is a science to setting up a beach chair. You want to face the sea, but not stare straight into the sun. You want the waves close enough to tickle your toes, but not so close that the pages of your "chick lit" get damp. However, when the beach you're setting your chair up on has a sand "cliff" that drops straight down several feet and ends close to the water's edge, your options are limited. My friend Evelyn and I planted

Tears, like the island's tropical storms, sometimes appeared out of nowhere, but we simply let them fall.

the backs of our chairs firmly against the sandy drop-off, put on our sunglasses, applied our sunscreen, and sat back to relax. So much for science.

Not five minutes later, I looked up from my book to see a huge wave bearing down on us. I glanced to my right and Evelyn, who used to be less than a foot away, was missing. My chair and I were still high and dry, firmly planted in the sand. But Evelyn was rolled up in a ball, complete with beach chair, and was tumbling down the beach and into the waves like the *Poseidon* cruise ship.

Come on, God! Haven't you picked on Evelyn enough? I tossed my complaints heavenward as I sprinted down the beach to help unfold my friend. From early on this whole dream vacation had crossed the line into a nightmare—for which I pretty much held God responsible. For months Evelyn and I had anticipated this trip to Hawaii. We'd traded a time-share and frequent flyer miles, taken time off work, sorted out the details of who'd handle all the car pools for our kids, and scrimped and saved. Finally, here was a chance for two harried moms to leave their cares behind and spend a whole week lounging and laughing.

Then a close friend of Evelyn's died unexpectedly. His memorial service was set for the morning we planned to leave. No amount of pleading with the airline could change our tickets. It was either go at the set time or forfeit the trip.

The morning of our departure felt more like a funeral than a vacation. Along with our swimsuits and sunscreen, we packed grief, loss, confusion, and what felt like betrayal by a God we deeply loved. Then, our connecting flight was delayed. One hour. Two hours. Six hours. Ten hours. Twelve . . . We could have gone to the funeral, taken a later flight, and still made it on our plane from Los Angeles to Oahu.

As the hours slowly dragged by, I kept glancing at my friend. She was quiet, distant. Her mouth was drawn in a straight, tight line. I was worried. Wondering how her heart was faring. Feeling responsible to try and protect her from getting hurt again. Trying to wrestle God's job right out from under Him, since He obviously seemed to have bigger concerns than cutting two weary moms a little vacation slack. Silently, I continued pleading with God, asking Him to comfort Evelyn, to hold her close, to work a miracle.

The only miracle I witnessed was when the airline provided coupons for a free meal. Evelyn and I headed to the closest fast-food establishment where we stocked up on grease, salt, fat, and caffeine. Evelyn stuck her fried apple pie in her carry-on, just in case we were still sitting at the airport gate in the wee hours of the morning. Almost. We boarded our flight shortly before midnight. Right after Evelyn discovered that her fried pie had been squished flat onto the pages of the magazine she'd brought to read on the plane.

Instead of reading, we slept. Or tried to sleep. My mind continued to pour out one long adolescent whine of prayer. When the flight attendant finally announced our descent into Oahu, I glanced at Evelyn. Asleep. Then I glanced out the window. Rain. I decided to keep the weather report to myself. Evelyn would find out soon enough.

As "luck" would have it, that moment came right after Evelyn discovered her luggage had not made the trip with us. Evelyn lifted her chin, looked me straight in the eye, took up her allegiance with Job, and said proudly, "We will not curse God and die."

Evelyn seemed to be doing fine. Perhaps I needed to start praying for me. My self-assigned role of "cruise director" for any and every journey—be it around the block or around the world—weighed heavily on me at that moment. All my carefully planned details were coming apart at the seams. Sad, soggy, sleep-deprived, and almost luggage-less, we stood in the dark waiting for a shuttle. Since we arrived on Oahu in the early morning hours, picking up our rental car and checking into our condo was out of the question. At least the airline provided a room at a nearby hotel for what remained of the night. I hardly remembered crawling beneath the sheets.

But dawn brought fresh hope. Sunlight poured through the white louvered shutters, along with a warm breeze scented by plumeria blossoms. The rain was gone. And so, we soon found out, was our reserved grade of rental car.

"I'm really sorry for the inconvenience," said the rental car agent as he walked us out to the lot, jingling a set of keys in his hand. "Perhaps this will do."

He was pointing to a cranberry red convertible.

OK, God, so the car was really a nice touch, but now You pick up Evelyn with a wave and try to send her out to sea! How come I stayed on the beach while she was pulled in? Remember, You're supposed to be helping her, healing her . . . Evelyn's laughter interrupted my runaway train of prayer.

Spitting saltwater and sand from her mouth while trying to untangle herself from the aluminum frame of the beach chair, Evelyn was laughing so hard she could barely breathe. She was a snarl of sandblasted limbs struggling to right herself while continuing to be pulled further down the shore with every oncoming wave.

"Three years from now how am I going to explain to my gynecologist why there is still sand in my Pap smear?" Evelyn choked out through laughter, tears streaming down her already salt-encrusted face.

By the time I'd helped Evelyn up, we were both laughing so hard that anyone watching would have assumed we were not completely in control of our faculties. And maybe they'd be right. For the first time on the trip, I'd truly let go, casting off the excess baggage I'd packed in my heart. I felt so much lighter. So much more like myself. More like who God created me to be.

Yet the irony of the moment wasn't wasted on either of us. There we'd sat, right next to each other. An unexpected wave sweeps one away and leaves one on the shore, untouched. If I were the one folded up in the beach chair, I'd have felt God had it in for me. But I wasn't. I was simply the friend. The onlooker.

No matter what an avid "cruise director" I happened to be,

God was the One who held a plan for Evelyn's life. She was in God's hands, not mine. As much as I wanted to comfort her, support her, and protect her, my place was to be her friend. Nothing more, nothing less. God, as always, was the only suitable Savior. And He provided a week of lounging and laughter after all. Tears, like the island's tropical storms, sometimes appeared out of nowhere, but we simply let them fall. God would dry them in His time, in His way. And His ways were so often wonderful.

My friend and I sat on beach chairs, planted firmly above our sandy drop-off, and read good books. We floated in an ocean cove on air mattresses—and so wished we'd taken Dramamine. We hiked through a tropical forest to take a dip in a "sacred" pool, only to discover our swimming companion was a rat the size of a Chihuahua. We ate cookies each night while watching the sunset and so much fresh pineapple that our tongues were raw. And we discovered that if we turned on the heater and drove fast enough, we could keep the convertible's top down through a storm.

But our days in paradise were numbered, at least this side of heaven. Evelyn and I packed our bags (yes, Evelyn's luggage did eventually show up) and headed back to the airport. We decided to check in our luggage early and then head down to the beach to take one last saunter on the shore.

We pulled up to the curb and I got out of the car to unload the bags. I was chatting away, when I noticed there was no response. I glanced at the driver's seat. Evelyn was missing. This time, there wasn't a wave in sight.

Anxiously scanning the sidewalk, I saw Evelyn standing by the main entrance, cradling a baby in her arms. "My baby, my baby isn't breathing!" cried the woman at Evelyn's side.

A siren's scream drowned out the mother's cries. I stood by our still running car, guarding our luggage, trying to see what was happening through the chaos of the growing crowd. Evelyn's face was down near the child's as the ambulance pulled up to the curb. Paramedics ran toward the scene. After handing the child to them,

Evelyn then turned to comfort the distraught parents nearby.

My friend, the nurse . . . I never even heard the initial cry of a frantic mom. But Evelyn had. A cry for help and Evelyn's years of experience and caregiver's heart kicked right in. Apparently the baby's breathing tube from a tracheotomy had clogged. When seconds mattered, Evelyn knew just what to do. And God had her there at just the right time.

It wasn't until later that it dawned on us: If our plane had not been delayed the week before, if we'd picked up the rental car at the original time, we would not have been there. We would have turned in the car first thing in the morning and been wandering around town until our plane left that evening.

Some cruise director I was. What I called disaster, God called opportunity. Only He could take the frayed threads of grief and discouragement and weave them into a striking tapestry of hope and healing. Now if I could just keep my hands off the loom . . .

You're blessed when you're at the end of your rope.
With less of you there is more of God and his rule.
Matthew 5:3 (*The Message*)

PERSONAL JOURNEY

WHAT kind of traveler are you? Are you a "cruise director," a follower, a fly-by-the-seat-of-your-pants kind of sojourner, or would you rather just stay home and avoid the hassle and risk altogether? What do you think this says about you?

CAN you think of a time when you tried to "wrestle God's job right out from under Him"? Why do you think you felt the need to try to control that situation?

DO you believe in coincidence, or do you feel every detail of life is directed by God's hand? Use Scripture to support your answer.

READ Jeremiah 29:11 and Romans 8:28. How can the truth of these two verses better enable you to surrender yourself, and those you love, to God?

WHAT area of your life is the most difficult to totally surrender to God? Take a few moments and talk to your loving Father about it. Is there anything you believe He wants you to do, to commit to, right now? If so, ask someone else to help hold you accountable in this area.

Journey Toward . . .
PURPOSE

Iona,

scotland

D eluge or downpour? Shower or squall? Was it coming in sheets, buckets, or cats and dogs? Washing the gullies or merely spitting, sprinkling, drizzling, or pitter-pattering on them? I sighed. No matter what the exact term happened to be for what the rain was doing, the fact that I'd spent the last three hours of our drive trying to categorize precipitation did not bode well for a fun-filled family vacation.

Right here, right now, I felt so at home on the path I'd chosen. In God's world, there are no "little things."

Half of our two-week trip through Scotland was over and we'd spent most of our time on winding one-lane roads dodging wet sheep. To make matters worse, my husband and our two teenagers were beginning to whine like bagpipes.

"You really should visit during the dry season," the storekeeper commented when we stopped to fill the rental van with gas.

"And when is that?" I asked.

She paused for a moment and then replied with a droll smile, "Now."

The Scottish Highlands had looked so inviting in the tour books: lush green glens, castles ringed by moats, ancient Viking ruins, and the mysteries of Loch Ness. Now, it was all crystal clear. Glens were green because they were continually bathed in storms of biblical proportions. Moats not only held off intruders but also the runoff from daily downpours. The Vikings came to pillage Scotland because their seafaring skills were as useful here on land as they'd been sailing over from Scandinavia. As for the legends of the Loch Ness monster? Too many inclement days can lead to too many pints in the pub.

But I continued to hold out hope like a soggy white flag. Today was the day I'd looked forward to for months. This afternoon I'd set foot on the tiny isle of Iona where the graves of 60 kings, including Macbeth's victim Duncan of Shakespearean fame, were found. At one time, the ground of Iona was considered so holy that it was reputed to remove the sins of anyone buried there. Guess Macbeth must have felt that could help clear up that whole murdering Duncan thing.

Known in the British Isles as the "cradle of Christianity," the spiritual heritage of Iona began with the arrival of Columba, a church leader who would later be declared a saint. In 563, Columba left his home in Ireland under rather questionable circumstances that may have included excommunication from the church and plagiarism resulting in exile. With a small band of fellow monks, Columba decided to begin a new life, and plant a new church community, on Iona because it was the first point from which he could no longer see Ireland. Columba's monastic community and zeal for sharing what he believed had a profound impact on the spiritual landscape of the British Isles and beyond.

My personal pilgrimage to Iona was fueled more by curiosity (and the fact that Iona was the name of my favorite Christian recording artist) than a desire to get up close and personal with holy dirt. But if this afternoon's weather happened to be a repeat of this last week, I'd be bringing home some holy boglike mud in the treads of my sneakers as a souvenir.

As we pulled up to the gate of our bed and breakfast, there was a momentary break in the clouds. My white flag of hope flew a little higher. Set free from the confines of the van, and the incessant chant of, "Keep to the left! Keep to the left!" on the road, we decided to take a brisk walk around the property.

Sheep to the right. Sheep to the left. We were surrounded by wet wool prancing on four legs. Staring at us like guard dogs without an ounce of courage or one hint of a clue, the sheep noisily bleated and baaed in a relentless drone. That's when my husband lost it. Perhaps it was too many hours in the car. Perhaps it was feeling cold and waterlogged for the last week. Perhaps it was simply Mark's inner child having been forced to wear a business suit for too many years. Whatever the reason, my usually dignified, intelligent, well-mannered husband ran at the sheep like a screaming banshee, flailing his arms and making unintelligible sounds at the top of his lungs. It was as if Mark were Godzilla and the sheep were countless Japanese movie extras. Fur balls scattered in every direction and the bleating increased to epic horror film proportions.

"What are you doing?" I yelled at my husband. "Sheep are high-strung! You're scaring them to death!'

"Yeah, Dad," my son, Ryan, chimed in. "They'll probably all have to be in therapy for years—all because of you!"

Mark looked at us with a satisfied grin. Perhaps even he didn't know why he did what he did. But one thing was certain. He sure enjoyed doing it.

We dropped our luggage off inside a cottage that overlooked the sea, had a quick snack, and then headed off to the ferry that would take us to Iona. As we left, the sheep were still bleating in a panicked chorus. My daughter, Katrina, got out of the van to close the sheep gate behind us. We made sure Mark was securely buckled into his seat. That twisted smile still hadn't left his lips.

But my concern for the herd's mental health quickly faded from mind as sunshine flooded through the windshield. The rain had not only stopped, but now the clouds were beating a hasty sheeplike retreat toward a distant horizon. Before us lay Iona, bathed in light.

If Ireland is the Emerald Isle, then Iona is the chip that broke free and floated north. Barely three miles long and less than a mile wide, the sliver of green glistened in its setting of a sapphire sea. Only a five-minute boat ride from the coast of Mull (the island we were currently on), the strait that separated the two islands is so narrow that people used to shout across it to summon the ferry. But we were in luck. The ferry was docked on our side and ready to load.

I instinctively walked toward the railing facing the stone abbey. The view was familiar, the picture I'd come to know from books and travel brochures. Though no structures remained from Columba's time, in the early 1200s a Benedictine abbey was built on the site of Columba's original monastery. While the abbey was rebuilt and restored several times, the adjacent nunnery lay in ruins.

Once we docked on Iona's shore, I headed off toward the ruins at a determined clip. I knew my family would be along sooner or later. They were enjoying the warmth of the sun and the scenic row of cottages facing a miniscule beach. I wanted a few minutes alone among the arches that led nowhere and cobbled half-walls to think, to pray, to listen to the stories the stones had to tell.

After a visit to Iona in 1773, Samuel Johnson wrote, "That man is little to be envied whose piety would not grow warmer among the ruins of Iona." I was anxious for my piety to be warmed, for my devotion to God to be stirred toward righteous action.

I wasn't a social activist or itinerant preacher. I was a wife and a mother, a middle-aged woman on vacation whose husband terrorized sheep. How did piety manifest itself in my life? In lieu of motivating monks and converting Celts, I was attempting to motivate teens and convert leftovers into palatable meals. Were my small acts as pious as Columba's dynamic ones? Could changing diapers or bedsheets be as holy an undertaking as changing the world?

I glanced back at my family, chatting, laughing, kicking stones along the graveled path. Certainly my world was larger than just the three of them. But they were my magnetic pole, the ones with the power to draw a vagabond mom back home time and time again. On occasion, I wondered where I'd be if I had remained single, if my beloved family was not part of my life. Would I be teaching English in Cambodia, working with the poor in India, perhaps even living a monastic life?

I recalled how as a little girl I'd visited a convent where Carmelite nuns lived behind closed doors. My grandmother had brought the gift of a warm meal, which was gratefully accepted with a smile but no words, by a willowy nun with a young, fresh face. My grandmother explained that the women inside had taken a vow of silence. She and the other women inside spent their days talking only to God.

At that moment I decided that was what I wanted to be when I grew up—someone who talked to God. I was only five or six at the time, and had probably never heard the word *piety,* but even then I longed for it. Looking back on that day in light of who I'd grown up to become, I couldn't imagine myself taking a vow of silence or even wearing the same thing every day. But talking to God? I had to smile. Here I was living out yet another childhood dream.

My life could have gone so many different directions, some more exotic, more exciting, more filled with spiritual and personal challenge. Perhaps on other paths I could have made a more visible mark on the world for God. But maybe that desire was really more about me than Him, more about me having to rely on seeing "results" to feel my life mattered. Was it enough to be faithful in the little things? I watched my family venturing off the gravel path to join me by the ruins—and felt a rush of contentment. Right here, right now, I felt so at home on the path I'd chosen. In God's world, there are no "little things."

My family and I wandered together through the tweed-stoned abbey. We talked about Columba and his followers and how their love of God caused them to do things that had an impact on the world—even right up to today. After all, Columba was the one who'd drawn us here.

We explored a field of Celtic crosses; the cemetery of kings; a shallow beach with smooth green stones instead of sand; a tiny town with roads but no cars; shop windows filled with tartans, shortbread, and religious doodads. I wondered what Columba would think if he returned to these shores today. I wondered if Samuel Johnson would believe piety could still be warmed among the kitsch. I wanted to assure him it could.

When we left Iona, the sun—once again—left Scotland. The next few days were a mélange of sheep, castles, and grassy green glens glazed in rain. But no rain fell where we now stood, beneath the streets of Edinburgh. Iona was light, color, faith. Here we were surrounded by dark shadowed despair. Like the ruins of Iona, the walls of Edinburgh had stories to tell. One of the most desperate tales was that of Mary King's Close.

In the seventeenth century, the Black Plague was an indiscriminant executioner. To try and keep the epidemic at bay, Edinburgh locked the gates of the city to outsiders. But rats never paid much mind to locks. There was an outbreak of the plague in Mary King's Close, a neighborhood where all the tenants' front doors opened onto an enclosed stairway (a "close") leading from the hilltop city down to the city walls. Each close had a gate at both the top and bottom of the staircase that was locked in the evenings for protection.

After the outbreak, the city leaders decided to try to contain the plague by refusing to reopen the locks with the morning light. It is believed that all 400 residents were trapped inside without access to food, water, or any medical care. Through the locked doors, the citizens of Edinburgh could hear the pleading cries of the men, women, and children of Mary King's Close. Day after day they grew weaker, fainter, until all was quiet. Today, the doors remain locked, a reminder of a sacrifice given by those who had no other choice than to give.

Empathy became my time machine. I pictured my own family locked behind that door. No food, no help, no hope. What would I do, say, pray? And what if my family had lived on the other side of the door? If I'd heard the cries for mercy or simply for a cool cup of water? What would I do, say, pray? What would piety, and God, ask of me?

As our tour ended, we returned to the streets of the twenty-first century that lay above the ghosts of the past. But I couldn't shake off the lives that had been lost below. The weight of the choices we make . . . to reach out or to withhold our help, our love, our faith from those around us. Perhaps Mary King's Close warmed my piety even more than Iona.

But right now, the only choice that lay before me was what kind of pizza to order. It sounded rather trite and superficial in light of what we'd just heard, but everyone was waiting on me, and that "everyone" included more than just my family. Rory and his girlfriend had just arrived to share our final "Scottish" lunch.

It had been a couple of years since Rory first knocked on our door in Colorado. He was selling encyclopedias. They were expensive. Probably out-of-date as soon as they were printed. Nothing I was interested in investing in. But as for the young man with the flurry of cropped curls and impish smile, that was a different matter.

His voice caught my attention much more than his words. His lilting accent said, "I'm far from home." I could relate to that feeling, so I asked him how he liked working here in the States. His smile drooped. He shared stories of not-so-welcome receptions at many front doors, of his loneliness, frustration, and exhaustion. I invited Rory to come back for a visit later that evening after his work was through.

So began a friendship. Over the next few weeks, Rory dropped by whenever his work brought him close to our neighborhood. And on his farewell visit, Rory presented Ryan (always a pushover for a great sales pitch) with his personal sample of his encyclopedia. Even after Rory returned to Scotland, we'd receive a long-distance call every now and then. Rory just checking in on his American "family." Now we were checking in on him.

As Rory animatedly chatted away, I thought of the difference one seemingly "little thing" had made. All I did was open the door—and then my heart. That choice was certainly not as earth-shattering as deciding whether or not to unlock the doors of Mary King's Close or share God's word in an often hostile, foreign land. But in God's grand scheme of life, I trusted that choice made a difference, even if I never had a chance to fully witness the results.

Maybe I *was* a social activist and itinerant preacher of sorts. And maybe God's purpose for my life was less like a job description and more like a chain of choices, a strong link being forged each time I chose God's way over my own. And maybe Scotland, even with the rain and wet sheep, was a place where my piety could not only be warmed, but set on fire.

> *Pray that our God will make you fit for what he's called you to be, pray that he'll fill your good ideas and acts of faith with his own energy so that it all amounts to something.*
> 2 Thessalonians 1:11 (*The Message*)

PERSONAL JOURNEY

THE word *pious* is not always viewed as something positive in today's society. Why do you think this is? How do you define piety? What has God used to "warm" you toward being more "positively" pious in your life?

WHAT are some "little things" that you've done just this week that in God's eyes may not be so little after all?

READ James 2:14–17. What relationship should faith and action have with one another? Consider your actions today. How has what you believe influenced what you've done?

WHAT is God's will, or purpose, for your life? Write out your own definition. Then read Romans 12:1–2; Ephesians 5:15–21; Philippians 2:13; and 1 Thessalonians 4:3. After reading these verses, do you want to revise your definition in any way?

IF your piety could still use a little warming, embark on a different kind of spiritual journey: Read an inspirational biography. Head to the library and pick up a book on Martin Luther King Jr., Henrietta Mears, Billy Graham, Lottie Moon, or anyone else who's inspired you to see how big God is and how through Him the "little things" we do can make a big difference.

Saint Petersburg,

Russia

B uilt like a bunker, her square shoulders testing the limits of her uniform's seams, her hair tightly bunned, the pursed-lipped security guard did not look happy. She waved her wand over Jim for the third time. The buzzer sounded again.

"Clean out pockets!" she ordered sternly. My friend Jim gave me a "what do I do now?" look. His wallet, change, keys and watch already lay on the table

I didn't see Lydia, or my skirt or turtleneck, again. So what to do with a wad of cash?

in front of him. In the pre-9/11 days of 1979, airport security was usually little more than a formality. But we were in the USSR before it split into independent states. The cold war was still on. Saint Petersburg was still Leningrad. And we were a rowdy group of students on spring break from college in Italy. I could tell Jim was beginning to sweat.

As Jim dug through his pockets one more time, a sheepish grin spread across his face. He held out a foil-wrapped chocolate Easter egg. Even the security guard cracked a smile. Crisis averted.

It wasn't the first we'd faced that day. In true Socialist style, our Russian airliner had no seat assignments. More troublesome, a large section of the plane had no windows. Instead, there were four small skylights in the ceiling, which might come in handy if the pilot practiced any stunt flying on our way into Leningrad. After a quick survey of the plane, that possibility sounded downright plausible.

Apparently we were flying less than economy. We were flying cargo—in what looked like a submarine with wings. Beneath us was a bare metal floor with a few carpet scraps tacked here and there to try hide the bolts that *secured* (and I use that term loosely) our folding seats to the body of the plane. There was no run-through of security procedures preflight. No demonstration of the proper use of emergency exits, oxygen masks, or life vests. That was probably because from what I could see, there were none. However, before takeoff the flight attendant did hand each passenger a complimentary motion sickness bag.

Once the pilot started the engine, the noise was so loud that conversation of any kind was out of the question. I glanced back at a group of my fellow students seated in the windowless section of the plane. They were flapping their arms in unison, obviously trying to do what they could to help get this jerry-rigged mass of metal off the runway and into the air. I was thankful God could hear my prayers over the engine's drone.

After surviving both the flight and airport security, we headed to our accommodations at the Youth Palace. Like "commercial jet" our "palace" didn't quite translate from Russian into English. We had to show the keys from our small, stark rooms to receive a towel and toilet paper each day. Breakfasts consisted of eggs with stacks of stale bread and large metal pots of tea. For both lunch and dinner we feasted on hunks of fat and potatoes in gravy, more stacks of stale bread, and glasses of water graced with prune pits, their furry prune pulp swaying like sea kelp every time I lifted my glass.

Yet the real culture shock lay outside our hotel. As my fellow students and I toured Leningrad and Moscow, our government-assigned guides provided lecture after lecture about the Soviet way of life, emphasizing its superiority over capitalist societies'. Socialism was repeatedly defined as a gift "to those according to their needs from those according to their abilities." Imperialism, on the other hand, was touted as "man taking advantage of man."

From my limited vantage point as a tourist, socialism appeared to me to be more like "equal opportunity poverty." Bleak rundown apartments filled the gray skyline. The country's largest department store bustled with people, but its shelves lay virtually empty. Customers waited outside in long lines for bread, only to be turned away at the bakery door because everything had been sold. I wanted to pack up the stacks of bread from the hotel and pass them out on the streets.

Although it was near the end of April, it was bitter cold. Icy pellets of snow came in frequent bursts, burning my face and turning my cheeks a dull purple. I'd heard that in Russia there are only two seasons: expectation and disappointment. After only one week, I discovered a third: resignation. The upside was that ice cream was readily available on street corners. The prescooped, flat-bottomed cones languished on tables, the vendors secure in the fact their goods wouldn't melt until July.

The only thing that was "hot" in Russia seemed to be the black market. For a country that denounced capitalism, undercover consumerism was thriving. At the airport, on the streets, in taxicabs, even in our hotel lobby, I was barraged with requests for "Jeans? Cigarettes? Gum?" One student in our group took full advantage of the situation by placing anything he could think of to sell in the clear plastic pocket of his backpack. He became a display case with legs. As for me, I didn't need to advertise. The black market came right to me.

I was in my hotel room getting ready for bed when I heard a timid knock. Before I could answer, two young women walked right in, giggling and shushing, while nervously glancing over their shoulder as they closed the door behind them. "Jeans?" they asked.

I froze. But my mind was racing. Here I was in my nightgown, fresh out of the shower, towel drying my hair. Not only was I speechless with surprise, I didn't want to get involved in anything illegal. I recognized one of the women as "Lydia" who worked in the hotel. I answered her with as polite a *"Nyet!* No!" as I could muster.

Lydia and her friend smiled. Then walked over and opened my suitcase. "Jeans?" they continued to ask.

I continued to *nyet.* I hadn't brought any jeans. And I didn't want to sell anything. When I'd entered the country, I'd exchanged a set amount of Italian lire for Russian rubles. For any purchase I made I received a receipt. When I left the country, I had to surrender the receipts and the remaining rubles—and the two better add up or I would be facing those security guards once again. The word *Siberia* flew through my mind.

That's when Lydia dug out my denim skirt. A reverent hush fell over the women. Lydia looked at what she held in her hands as though it were the crown jewels of a Russian czar. Then she looked up at me. "How much?"

One again, I was speechless. Lydia handed me a pad and a pen. "How much?" she repeated. I felt trapped, unsure of what to do. I knew what I wanted to do—escort these women out the door. But without knowing Russian, without being able to explain myself, that seemed so rude. I made a snap decision. Remembering a friend down the hall who'd sold a pair of jeans for the equivalent of $100, I wrote that amount on the pad.

Lydia held her hand to her mouth and gasped. Now, I'd offended her. Well, not quite. Lydia reached back into my suitcase and pulled out a turtleneck sweater. Holding it up with the skirt, Lydia then reached for a wad of rubles stashed in the waistband of her pants. As she counted off bill after bill I started to sweat. I always had been a pushover for door-to-door sales. But this time I'd gone too far. I pictured myself in Siberia, without even a turtleneck to keep me warm.

Lydia put her finger to her lips. "Shhh!" she said emphatically. She ran her finger quickly across her throat and stuck out her tongue. Even without knowing Russian, I got the message loud and clear. Then giggling once more, the women quickly exited my room with their newfound treasures. I stood silent, a stack of rubles in my hand. Ashamed.

How easily I'll sell myself, God! Why didn't I just let them take what they wanted? Why didn't I just give them those things for free? That skirt was from Kmart! I bet I didn't pay more than 30 bucks for the whole lot. I have so much and everyone here has so little. What's wrong with me? Am I more ashamed of what I did or more worried I'll get caught? I don't even know. I'm so sorry, God. What should I do, what should I do?

I knew in an instant. I'd give the money back. Somehow I'd convey to Lydia she could keep the clothes. I opened the door and looked down the hall. The two women were nowhere in sight.

Tomorrow, Lord. Tomorrow I'll find Lydia and make everything right again . . .

The next day I asked a friend for one of the rosaries she'd brought into Russia to give away. Throughout our trip, Elaine had given rosaries to strangers on the street. In a city with 3,000 libraries and only 18 open churches, her gift was usually met with surprise, and often tears.

Though I attended Catholic Mass as a child, I hadn't held a rosary in my hand for years. I didn't feel I needed beads to pray to God, but I couldn't think of any other way to let Lydia know that God was the reason I wanted to return her money. I wrapped the rosary around the bills and put them in my purse, hoping to run into Lydia in the hotel so I could return to her what I felt was hers.

But I never had the chance. I didn't see Lydia, or my skirt or turtleneck, again. So what to do with a wad of cash? The night before our return to school in Italy, I decided to treat a few of my friends to a dinner of more than fat à la gravy. And what a dinner it was. We took our seats in a cavernous room where shadows and cigarette smoke mingled together, creating an aura of intrigue by candlelight. Before me were four glasses, three sets of silverware, three plates, and mountains of food—with not one slice of stale bread in sight.

To the sound of balalaikas and mandolins, my friends and I dined on salmon, pâté in pastry, roast beef, carrots and cabbage, chicken salad, sliced tongue, blini (pancakes), roast oxen with scallions, mounds of caviar, layered cake, meringue cookies, and ice cream. Between courses we were offered thimble-sized swigs of vodka to cleanse our palates.

By the end of the evening, many of the other patrons seemed to have more than their palates cleansed. Groups of men rose from their tables to join the singers and dancers that had performed during the meal. They locked arms and danced around the room in a boisterous, bouncing line. Soon the dance looked more like a child's game of "crack the whip," with the last man in line, holding an almost empty bottle of vodka high in the air, being pulled between the tables at breakneck speed.

It was a memorable end to a memorable week. And after almost 30 years, those memories still give me pause. Things have changed in Russia. Things have also changed in me. Today if I faced the same situations, would I do things differently? How would I respond to Lydia? Would I still wind up at a lavish dinner with my friends?

God has given me so much. So many adventures. So many

chance meetings. So many resources. So many opportunities to shine His light into the lives of others struggling to find their way. I can hear my own words to my children replaying in my head: "With privilege comes responsibility." I know my heavenly Father would agree. And today when I ask Him, "What should I do, what should I do?" He tells me to tell my story. So that's what I do.

> *From everyone who has been given much, much*
> *will be demanded; and from the one who has been*
> *entrusted with much, much more will be asked.*
> Luke 12:48 (NIV)

PERSONAL JOURNEY

HOW would you have responded if Lydia showed up at your door? Why?

CONSIDER the words of Luke 12:48. What has God entrusted you with "much" of? Knowledge? Wealth? Freedom? Material goods? Talents? Influence? How can you use what God's entrusted you with more generously or responsibly?

READ Matthew 25:31–46. What part of Jesus's parable resonates most deeply in your heart? Is there anything God is asking you to do?

YOU cannot travel far without crossing paths with someone who is less fortunate than you are in one way or another. Read Deuteronomy 15:11; Proverbs 19:17; 31:20; and

1 Corinthians 13:3. What motivates you to reach out to those in need? What do you feel is your God-given responsibility in this area? Spend some time in prayer over the verses you've just read and consider what your response to those in need should be.

IF there is anything in your life that you feel you need to "make right," don't wait any longer. Ask God what you should do. Then do it!

Pikes Peak,
Colorado

*O*K, God, what is it with me and mountains? Why can't I just take a photo at the bottom and call it good? Pikes Peak even has a road to the top, not to mention its own cog railway; so why, oh why, am I walking up it? By what stretch of my imagination did I think this sounded "fun"? I must be crazy. Crazy, oxygen-deprived, and a very slow learner . . .

Anyone who says hiking is a good way to clear your mind must never have

"I don't know if I can make it," I confessed, my eyes now down-cast and my own impetuous smile long gone.

spent any time within a cerebral cortex like mine. Inside, a constant barrage of questions and complaints was being lobbed at both God and me. Outside, it was way too quiet. I was afraid the soft crunch of boots on the trail, the occasional songbird, and the shiver of the wind rustling through the aspen trees might not be enough to hide the sound of my own breathing. A sound reminiscent of a swimmer gasping for air as she goes down for the last time.

If Lori heard my gulps and gasps, she was politely trying to ignore them. Her blonde head bobbed up and down in front of me, step after steep, uphill step. Lori not only didn't seem winded, she seemed downright perky. Eight miles down, four to go!

Maybe that's what it's like to be 23. It's hard to remember that far back anymore . . . Just like it was hard to remember Lori and I weren't "peers" in a chronological sense. We'd been friends for several years, meeting for coffee, singing together at church, chatting about every topic that happened to enter our heads. And for the last several months we'd been rising before the sun to take a brisk 2½-mile walk along a mountain stream. We'd seen deer, rabbits, beavers, and each other without makeup—both literally and figuratively.

Somehow, walking side by side, instead of looking into each other's eyes as we would in a typical conversation, seemed to open a fresh vein of honesty. We rejoiced. We grieved. We prayed. We grappled over things that didn't seem to fit into a tidy little box of Christian faith. Sometimes we disagreed. But what we seemed to do most was encourage one another toward becoming the women God created us to be. We may have started walking to get our bodies in shape, but it was our souls that wound up getting the most beneficial workout.

It was on our morning walk that the idea arose to celebrate Lori's upcoming birthday with a hike up "the peak." But it wasn't until we were on our way up Barr Trail that I asked Lori what birthday she was celebrating. I was well aware she was younger than me, but her answer of "23" caught me by surprise. I was twice Lori's age. She was half of mine. I could be her mother. . . . Whatever way I expressed it, it didn't sound any better. I felt a sudden onset of osteoporosis.

Of course when we'd started our birthday hike, there had been three of us. Donna, the third member of our morning trio (a new friend whose age lay somewhere between Lori's youth and my decline), had started off almost as perky as Lori. But ill-fitting shoes, burgeoning blisters, and bleeding toes reduced Donna to tears at Barr Camp, the halfway point along the nearly 13-mile trek to the top.

Donna decided her only choice was to limp her way back down. Lori and I were torn. Should we abandon our friend or abandon our birthday quest to the top? Weather reports via radio at Barr Camp added to our dilemma. Intermittent snow showers and 30 mph winds currently wrapped the summit in near blizzard conditions. I surveyed the clear blue sky above me and the 70°F temperatures around me. The peak itself was obscured from our point on the trail, but I knew what was true at 10,000 feet didn't necessarily hold true at 14,000. Welcome to fall in the Rockies.

We talked with other hikers at Barr Camp. They too were torn. Some headed back down the trail, while others continued on toward the summit. Donna contacted her husband via cell phone and he agreed to hike up and meet her along the trail. She encouraged Lori and me to go on without her. She didn't want to hold us back.

Lori and I looked each other in the eye. If our concern over Donna wasn't enough to make us turn around, perhaps common sense should have been. But an impetuous smile fleeted across our lips. There was something about a challenge that taunted us. Perhaps it made me feel 23 again, who knows? Whatever it was, we bid Donna Godspeed as she hobbled off down the trail. Then Lori and I enthusiastically set off toward the summit.

Of course that was a couple of miles and innumerable switchbacks ago. Back when I could still breathe. "I've got to rest for just a minute," I panted. Lori stopped, casually leaned against a rock, and smiled.

"I don't know if I can make it," I confessed, my eyes now downcast and my own impetuous smile long gone. "I feel like I'm holding you back. I should have gone down with Donna. What if the weather's bad? What if we almost make it to the top and we have to turn around and walk all the way back down?"

"If we have to turn around, we will," Lori said. "But we're not to that point yet. Let's just see how far we can go."

"But I don't want to walk farther up if it means we can't catch a ride from the top down," I said, starting to sound decidedly whiny. "OK, God!" I shouted at the top of my voice to the now cloud-covered skies. "We need to know now! Should we keep going?"

In that instant, the sun sliced through the clouds with a vibrant burst of light and warmth as a patch of blue opened up above our heads.

"I think that's a yes!" I said with a laugh and a disbelieving shake of my head.

"Come on, you're doing great! Why don't you go first, so I can follow your pace?" Lori replied. The decision was made. It wasn't time to quit. At least not as long as Lori was by my side. Mile after grueling mile she acted as cheerleader, personal trainer, and counselor to the aged. Anytime I began to lag, Lori was my second wind.

If only Inestine B. Roberts had had a Lori. Inestine died on Barr Trail, close to where we were now, back in 1957. She was 87 years old (although her memorial plaque erroneously states she was 88), which meant I was almost half her age. Although this was her 14th ascent of Pikes Peak, Inestine made a fatal mistake. Upset over a disagreement, she decided to head back down the mountain alone. Right above timberline she tripped, injured herself, and wound up dying of exposure.

As we passed Inestine's plaque, I thought of Donna. She'd called (hurray for cell phone coverage on Pikes Peak!) to say she'd made it home OK with her husband's help. I was glad she was safe and also glad I hadn't quit. After all, the summit was in sight. I only wished there were three of us here to celebrate.

But Lori and I couldn't celebrate yet. The 16 Golden Stairs stood between us and the warm doughnuts waiting at the Summit House.

A half mile of poetically—yet inaccurately—named switchbacks, not stairs, loomed before us. And the only flakes I saw were made of snow, not gold.

A true blizzard hadn't materialized, but the searing cold wind and ice-packed trail made the going even slower than before, something I would have previously thought impossible. Lacking gloves, I grabbed my extra pair of hiking socks and put them on my hands. Not only did they serve as makeshift mittens, but as sock puppets that narrated the final steps of our grueling ascent. Looking back, I can only blame it on the lack of oxygen.

Inching our way up the icy trail, every step forward slid halfway back. Exertion and a lack of oxygen brought most of our conversation to a halt. We communicated mainly through glances that asked, "Are you hanging in there?" and nods that replied, "I'm right here with you." We celebrated the milestone of each switchback with a grin and a sock puppet high five.

After what felt like a mile spent in slow motion, the final switchback was behind us. Lori and I could now measure our goal in feet, instead of miles. That's when Lori did something I'll never forget. She grabbed my hand and pulled me up next to her on the trail. "We're crossing this finish line together," she said. And we did.

A half million people travel to the summit of Pikes Peak every year. Only 15,000 of them attempt to make the journey on foot. Many of those who start turn back before they make it to the top. I would have been one of them if it hadn't been for the encouragement of a friend.

God knew from the start that it wasn't good for man, or woman, to be alone. It took me a while longer to catch on. But looking over my life, and at the mountains of fear, shame, and blame I've had to climb, one thing remains constant. God has brought people into my life to walk by my side, to encourage me toward the summit. All I need to do is grab their hands, open my heart, and keep on putting one foot in front of the other.

> *Gently encourage the stragglers, and reach out for*
> *the exhausted, pulling them to their feet.*
> 1 Thessalonians 5:14 (*The Message*)

PERSONAL JOURNEY

WHICH decision would you have made at Barr Camp: Would you have returned with Donna or continued on toward the summit? Why?

TO encourage others means to give them hope or confidence or to share some of your courage with them. Whose encouragement has made a difference in your life? What did that person do or say that was so significant?

NOT everyone has the gift of encouragement, but that doesn't mean you can't become an encourager. Ask God to show you how He can use your unique gifts and personality to help lift others up when they need it most.

READ Romans 15:4. One reason God gave us Scripture was to encourage us. Give an example of how God's Word has encouraged you.

ASK God to bring one person to mind who is in need of encouragement. Then pray about the best way you can share some of your courage with him or her this week.

Luxor,

Egypt

A bloodcurdling scream is an effective alarm clock. I jumped out of bed and ran across the hall to Janet's room, the epicenter of my early morning wake-up call. The screams were now coming in spurts. So was the banging emanating from her bathroom. I peeked inside.

"Cockroaches!" my friend managed to utter through her hysteria. Janet pulled the hastily wrapped bath towel a little tighter around her shivering body. "When I turned

But our guide was well aware tourists did not travel this far to hear about the living. They were drawn to Egypt by the dead.

on the shower, they all came charging out of the drain." Janet's screeches began to subside as the young boy who stood guard outside our rooms at night continued pummeling errant beetles with his shoe.

A word to the wise: Never travel economy in Egypt. Of course, advice like that only comes through the benefit of hindsight. That's something college students usually have little of. Something else they have little of—even those studying abroad—is money. Hence my friends and I opted to downgrade the "moderate" accommodations recommended by our Italian travel agent to "budget." Luckily we elected not to do the same with our train ticket to Luxor.

After checking out of our roach motel (unfortunately not before my blow dryer blew a circuit, throwing the entire establishment into darkness), my three friends and I hailed a taxi to Cairo's railway station. We emerged from the fake fur-lined cab into a wave of pushing, shouting, clamoring confusion. Attempting to squeeze into the fast moving tide of people flowing toward the single-entry door on the train, Janet and Dale went one direction while Jeannie and I went the other. My roommate and I traded nervous smiles. Jeannie had been my closest companion ever since our arrival in Florence three months ago. Soft-spoken and on the timid side, but a faithful and fun-loving friend, I'd convinced Jeannie a trip to Egypt would be the ultimate fall break adventure. I wondered if she was having second thoughts. Or thirds, by this point.

Using our luggage as a shield, Jeannie and I made our way through the train's economy seating. Men, women, children, sheep, chickens, and suitcases were piled under, over, and around aging wooden benches. The accommodations resembled a boxcar for livestock. I began praying Jeannie and I would still be on speaking terms by the time we returned to school. But our "sleeping car" yielded a pleasant surprise. We had a private compartment sporting two fold-up beds, a fold-up sink, and a picture window that actually opened and closed. Feeling a bit like Pharaoh among the Israelites, we settled in.

The train to Luxor jiggled and jostled its way down the tracks through the night. Luckily neither Jeannie nor I wanted to sleep.

Our window was like a movie screen, showing a first-run film of *The Land by the Nile*. Chaotic Cairo did a slow fade into mile after mile of silent sand. Children ran through furrowed fields chasing water buffalo. Huddled by a fire, a young boy read a book while the family's camel looked on. A fiery sunset turned palm trees and small villages into a velvet Elvis-styled backdrop, vibrant reds highlighting inky black silhouettes.

As the hour grew late, Jeannie and I dressed for bed. But we continued to stare out into the night, straining our eyes to find unfamiliar treasures hidden in the darkness of the desert. When our train unexpectedly slowed, then came to a stop, Jeannie and I pushed our noses up toward the window. We peered into the nearly impenetrable night with even more intensity.

"Look!" I said. "Fireflies!"

Small flickers of light began to gather by our window. They would glow brightly, fade, then begin to burn brightly again.

"Cigarettes!" Jeannie shouted, pulling the curtain across the window with one swift yank. It seemed the passengers waiting at the remote train station were as interested in checking us out as we were in the landscape. That was our signal to head to bed. Our 6:00 A.M. arrival in Luxor meant little time for sleep.

Cairo had felt like another world. . . . The airport "welcoming committee" of soldiers holding machine guns adorned with glistening bayonets. Helter-skelter traffic rampaging through a grid of streets like cockroaches fleeing a flooded drain. An all-night chorus of singsong Arabic echoing through neighborhoods that refused to sleep. Hawkers pushing a camel ride around the Pyramids—then charging riders an additional fee to dismount the beast at the end.

Luxor felt like another time. We traded our train compartment for one of the horse-drawn buggies, the only taxis in town. The Western-style dress so prevalent in Cairo was gone. Instead, long caftans and pointy-toed elf shoes were the norm. *Feluccas*, their single sails resembling worn bedsheets billowing in the breeze, glided over the surface of the Nile. A thin, fertile green border lined the banks of the river, ending abruptly in sand, sand, and yet more sand. The barren nothingness of desert continued far beyond what my eye could see.

Our hotel arose like a modern mirage, out of place against the tiny packed-earth houses that lined the outskirts of town. Though I enjoyed the quaint surroundings, I had to admit I was looking forward to a beetle-free bedroom. But sleep would come later. A quick breakfast and we were off again, reunited with our fellow students, and ready to take in the sights Luxor had harbored for centuries.

Our guide provided a nonstop succession of rapid-fire facts as we bounced down a dirt road in one of the few cars I'd seen. He spoke about life in Luxor, once known as Thebes. But our guide was well aware tourists did not travel this far to hear about the living. They were drawn to Egypt by the dead.

Certainly I was. From middle school right on through college, any time I could work ancient Egypt into the topic of an assigned paper, I did. The quest for life after death through mummification, the lavish burial process, and the practice of pulling the innards of royalty out through their nostrils with a hook (and then storing their organs in fancy jars) had always sent my already revved-up imagination into overdrive.

I'd visited the famed Pyramids near Cairo 5 years earlier with my parents. But we'd never made it as far as the Valley of the Kings. Today that site of 62 ancient tombs (62 discovered so far, that is) lay just a few miles away. When the Great Pyramids of Giza were built, they proved to be a giant X in the sand for treasure hunters. After the tombs' riches were looted, and their mummies "robbed" of the afterlife they'd striven so hard to attain, Egypt's future rulers were buried more clandestinely. One of those rulers was King Tutankhamen.

King Tut's tomb in the Valley of the Kings is undoubtedly its most celebrated site. And it's not because the king who died in his late teens was such a phenomenal Pharaoh; until Howard Carter opened the tomb in 1922, it had remained undisturbed for over 3,000 years. The lavish artifacts inside have since toured the museums of the world. I'd seen them first in the Cairo museum 5 years before. But the archaeologist inside me wanted a closer look. She wanted to poke her nose inside the tomb, to walk where kings walked, to ponder the lengths people would go to seek eternal life. That's why I'd dragged my poor roommate to the land the Israelites longed to flee.

But before we made our way through the desert to the Valley of the Kings, our guide had scheduled another stop. As the car's tires ground to a halt, three figures caught my eye. The first was a scarecrow (dressed like a sheik) guarding a field. The other two were stone. Seated side-by-side, the two 75-foot figures of Amenhotep III looked ready to crumble to the ground. Faces missing, chunks of stone gone from their timeworn arms and legs, I was afraid to venture too close for fear of falling appendages. But this pair had battled sand storms, the scorching sun, and the rise and fall of the Nile for almost 2,500 years. Chances are they'd remain upright at least until lunchtime.

I stood before the Colossi of Memnon with poetry running through my head. My high school English teachers would have been so proud. I knew the source was "Ozymandias," but the only words I could recall were "two vast and trunkless legs of stone." For a kid with dreams of lost cities and ancient civilizations, the words of Percy Bysshe Shelley's poem had formed a picture that embedded itself permanently within my gray matter.

Supposedly, these colossi inspired Shelley to pen "Ozymandias." Hmmm. These guys seemed to have both trunks and legs, albeit tattered ones. The funny thing was, Shelley's words had run through my head 5 years earlier when I'd traveled with my parents to Memphis, Egypt's ancient capital city. There I'd seen a gargantuan statue toppled in the sand. It's true he was also a legless trunk, not trunkless legs, but Shelley's words had hit me then as they did now.

I didn't know back then that the guy in Memphis was Ramses II— or as he was called in Greek, Ozymandias. In my mind, and perhaps in Shelley's, all of Egypt told the tale of Ozymandias. From the Colossi of Memnon to Memphis to the monoliths of Abu Simbel and beyond, statue after statue depicted the image of someone once admired, even worshipped. Someone of great power and position. Someone whose stone visage remained centuries after his physical body had returned to dust.

Yes, a few of these ancient celebrities retained their royal following by becoming curiosities ogled over in museums. But even an intact mummy with all the riches a Pharaoh could ever want couldn't guarantee these once flesh-and-blood people what they longed for. They wanted a door that would lead them into another world, a life that would outlast their images carved in stone, a key that held the secret to immortality. They wanted what I had.

I shivered, despite the warmth of the desert sun. The treasure of the Pharaohs was mine. Eternal life was a gift extended to me by a King.

I hadn't deserved it, earned it, or even ransacked it from a royal tomb. All I did was say yes when I heard God call my name. "Yes, I believe You are who You say You are. Yes, I'm sorry for turning my back on You for so long. Yes, I choose to follow wherever You lead."

Before Ramses II, before Amenhotep III, and long before me, there was a man named Moses who said yes to God. He brought news of an almighty King to the Pharaoh (who many scholars believe to be Amenhotep II), but Egypt's ruler chose to put his faith in his own royal power and riches. The gift of immortality was within his reach, but instead Pharaoh chose a future as solid as the desert's shifting sand. Moses was a witness to what God did next. And I'm a witness too. A witness to the personal Red Seas God has held back for me.

For long after the Colossi of Memnon fall to the ground, the Pyramids disappear into a pile of dust, and the Nile itself refuses to flow, my life, like Moses's, will continue—in the company of an eternal King.

> *"I, even I, am the LORD, and apart from me*
> *there is no savior. I have revealed and saved and*
> *proclaimed—I, and not some foreign god among*
> *you. You are my witnesses," declares the LORD,*
> *"that I am God. Yes, and from ancient days I am*
> *he. No one can deliver out of my hand."*
> Isaiah 43:11–13 (NIV)

PERSONAL JOURNEY

JOHANN Wolfgang von Goethe said, "Life is the childhood of our immortality." What truth do these words hold about today? About eternal life?

READ Romans 6:23; John 3:16; and Ephesians 2:8–9. What is our (as well as the Pharaohs'!) barrier to immortality? What is the key that opens the door to another world?

YOU are a firsthand witness to what God has done in your life. Every time you read the Bible, you're also a witness to what God's done in the past. How does being a witness play a part in your everyday life?

DO you believe God's gift of eternal life can be taken away from you? Write down three verses that support what you believe.

HAVE you ever wholeheartedly said yes to the King? If not, what's holding you back? Spend some time talking to God about what it means to give Him authority over every kingdom, both big and small, in your life.

Churchill,

Canada

Your nose is turning white!" the musher's voice was barely audible through the fur-rimmed tunnel of my snowsuit hood. But his actions sure caught my attention. He shoved one of his gloves in his pocket, then reached for my nose with his semiwarm hand. Tightly pinching my nostrils together with his fingers, all circulation and airflow to my frosted snout came to a halt.

All I could do was pray my nose wasn't

*Four seconds.
I'd traveled
thousands of miles
for four seconds.
The crazy thing was,
it was worth it.*

running at the time. But how could I tell? All my extremities had turned to blocks of ice—which made the fact that I was still standing upright, my gargantuan snow boots balanced one behind the other on the thin metal rail behind a fast-moving dogsled, all the more incredible.

"Go on by!" the musher called out to the dogs harnessed in front of us. They yanked us fast then slow, up then down, tilting, swaying, slicing, and sliding up over rocks, around trees, down through gullies, and over snowfields of frozen tundra. It reminded me of riding an elephant in Thailand—only at a breakneck pace, with Eskimo Pies® for hands and feet, and dressed in an arctic excursion suit that could have earned me an audition for Sumos on Ice. But at -27°F, not including windchill, frostbite took precedence over fashion.

With one hand on my nose and the other on the hand bow, the musher continued to steer the sled back toward the warming hut. I continued to try to breathe through my mouth air that could have flash frozen a piece of salmon before you could say "Iditarod." Did I mention I also had several cups of tea before we left? Let's just say that the snack of warm moose meat that awaited my return was not as welcome a sight as the outhouse. Well, at least in theory.

When I yanked open the ice-coated wooden door, I found half a snowman waiting for me on the toilet seat. There was also a small drift on the toilet paper roll. A movie scene where a kid gets his tongue stuck to an icy pole played in my head.

If I sit down will I . . .? I refused to let my mind wander any farther. Desperate times call for desperate measures.

Just ask any one of the 900 residents who call Churchill, Canada, their year-round home. Located on the lower edge of Hudson Bay, a 2½-hour flight north of Winnipeg, there are no roads to Churchill. You can only get here by plane, train, and during the summer months, boat. The town is six blocks long and two blocks wide, and during polar bear season folks don't walk outside the middle two blocks without toting a firearm. I bet none of the locals would think twice about a little snow on their seats.

Of course, none of the locals seemed to mind if there was no running water between January and the spring thaw. Or that fresh vegetables are available so infrequently that their arrival is announced on the local TV station. Or that the average winter temperature is about -25°F, often dropping to -50°F with windchill. Or that mascara freezes right off your lashes onto your face, leaving you looking like a frostbitten raccoon.

Why would anyone in his or her right mind choose to live here? I wondered.

After successfully returning to the warming hut, I posed my question to the 20-something "local" who'd whipped up the moose meat. An ecobiology major, Carrie spent her early adulthood wandering the wilderness of western Canada. She settled down for a while and opened a restaurant in an abandoned boat on an island off the coast. Using tree stumps for tables and chairs, she and a friend served their own blends of tea and baked goods. They lived in a one-room cedar house without the benefit of electricity or running water. And she loved it.

"But not as much as here," Carrie continued, her expression bubbling over with enthusiasm. "In only three more months wildflowers will be in bloom everywhere!" Then Carrie returned to stoking the crude wood-burning stove so she could boil enough water to wash my worn plastic teacup.

I guess people choose to live here for the exact same reason my sister, her husband, and I longed to visit. Beauty, unbridled beauty. Some come for the wildflowers. Some for the beluga whales that fill Churchill Bay every summer. Others for the adventure of being in the polar bear capital of the world. As for me, I was lured by the promise of catching a glimpse of the northern lights (aurora borealis).

There were no guarantees. Sometimes they showed, sometimes they didn't. Sometimes the night sky was concealed by clouds, as it had been the night before. My first night. My first chance. And my first very brief glimpse.

I'd stood outside off and on for hours, my neck craned toward the heavens. I eyed every small break, every momentary parting in the clouds in hope of seeing a flash of light. My feet were so cold I feared that when I took off my boots I'd find toes rolling around like frozen peas in my socks.

But then I saw it. Rollicking ribbons of light in a small patch of night. A squiggle of pink, and then green, raced by like a Precambrian sea creature glowing beneath ocean waves as dark as the midnight sky. Then the lights were gone. Hidden once more behind a wall of clouds.

Four seconds. I'd traveled thousands of miles for four seconds. The crazy thing was, it was worth it. Even if the next three nights revealed nothing more, I could go home happy. Who was I to question the sanity of the people who chose to live here year-round?

But tonight offered a second chance. Like a kid who'd just had her first taste of ice cream, I was already hungry for more. Could I live without it? Sure. But if tonight God was offering seconds, why not enjoy?

By 4:00 P.M., the sun had already dropped behind the horizon, leaving everything bathed in a warm, pink glow. The sky was clear, the air cold enough to steal my breath. Dressed in layer upon layer, and sworn off tea in any form, I rolled my well-insulated self into the van for the drive to a cabin somewhere off the main road. With our guide, Cindy, Lee, three other adventurers, and me all dressed in excursion suits and toting camera equipment, tripods, binoculars, hats, gloves, scarves, extra socks, and blankets, we resembled frat boys trying to test the capacity of a phone booth. But anticipation acted like a shoehorn. We squeezed ourselves in with little regard for comfort or personal space.

Outside the van, space was one thing that wasn't in short supply. Vast, flat snowfields flecked with a few stunted evergreens stretched for mile upon mind-numbing mile. Isolation is probably more brutal than the cold for those who call this place home.

That's probably why an *inukshuk* marks the edge of town. In Inuktitut, the language of the indigenous Inuit people, *inukshuk* means the "likeness of a person." It's a pile of rocks stacked to resemble a human figure with arms pointing out across the barren landscape. These manmade monuments are used to help point the way toward good fishing and hunting, to warn of impending danger, or to point travelers toward the nearest settlement. In the traditional Inuit culture, men often spent hours alone hunched over a small hole in the ice waiting for a seal to surface. Sometime an inukshuk was built simply to remind these men they were not alone.

In the van, I didn't need an inukshuk to remind me of that fact. My companions and I bounced into and off of one another as we bumped along a partially paved, pothole-pocked road. "Look!" someone shouted. We all merged to one side of the van, trying to press our faces against the ice-frosted windows. Even before we made it to the cabin, the aurora borealis had come out to play. "Faster, faster," I urged the driver under my breath, afraid that the lights would fade before I could get a good look. Afraid that my "one taste" really would have to be enough. But tonight God would provide an entire light buffet.

It's hard to describe in words what light does when it dances through the fingers of a playful God. From a scientist's point of view, the northern lights (and the southern lights for that matter) are merely an electric discharge that results when the earth's magnetic field "excites" particles from the sun's solar winds. But science can't explain why your heart goes wild at the sight.

Where last night our mini light show featured highly caffeinated neon doodles, tonight we watched rolling waves of soft green swirls. Last night they rumbaed. Tonight, they waltzed. The waves appeared out of nowhere in any and every direction. I'd catch them out of the corner of my eye and before I could fully turn my head, they'd be gone. One minute they're puffs of smoke. The next, tornado-like funnels reaching toward the ground. They're Chinese dragons in a New Year's parade. Living watercolors painting a masterpiece in the sky. God playing with His Etch-A-Sketch of light.

For more than 300 nights a year, the northern lights are on display above Churchill. That's because the location lies beneath the Van Allen (radiation) belt where the polar aurora is most visible. And on the other side of the world, the southern lights (aurora australis) perform a show of their own. Aerial photography has revealed how the aurora borealis and the aurora australis are often mirror images of each other, sweeping and swaying like dance partners keeping step on opposite sides of the globe. My mind savored the possibilities of permanent residence in such a place. A place where I could never lose sight of divine magic. *If I lived here, how could I ever sleep? I'd always be afraid of missing the show outside!*

But how long would that last? Chances are as the months wore on I'd grow weary of waiting, watching, shivering, chattering, shaking, oohing, and aahing. Tired of seeing my breath create its own frosty trails in the night. Wasn't one reason I longed to see the aurora borealis because I'd become rather complacent with the other wonders in the heavens? Orion, Cassiopeia, the moon, the Milky Way, even an occasional meteor shower felt rather common and predictable. Who was I kidding? One reason I was always traveling, always seeking new landscapes, was because I craved a fresh "fix" of adventure and beauty. Home could no longer support my habit.

Though the light show continued, cold, exhaustion, and perhaps the first hint of boredom, drew us all back to the van. It was well past midnight. We rode home in silence as wisps of smoky white light played "hide-and-seek" in the heavens.

Morning seemed to arrive shortly after I'd thawed. While my sister and her husband went on to breakfast, I decided to spend some quiet time in God's presence. On vacation, I often read through the Book of Psalms, matching each psalm's number to the day of the month. February 19 . . . I turned to Psalm 19 and began to read:

The heavens declare the glory of God; the skies proclaim the work of his hands. Day after day they pour forth speech; night after night they display knowledge. There is no speech or language where their voice is not heard. Their voice goes out into all the earth, their words to the ends of the world. (Psalm 19:1–4 NIV)

I couldn't see verse 5. My eyes were too filled with tears.

I'd been wrong all along. It wasn't beauty that drew me to Churchill.

It wasn't even adventure. It was truth. God's truth. On display night after night. Here I was in Churchill, at the end of the world, and God's voice—through the work of His hands—was declaring His glory and knowledge in a language that needed no words.

When Cindy and Lee returned from breakfast, I couldn't contain my excitement. "Listen to what I just read!" I said, reading the psalm aloud. Both Cindy and Lee were so moved by the words they asked me to read them again. I didn't need to say anything more. God's truth spoke so clearly the night before Cindy commented, "You've got to share that with our guide!"

But the next time I saw our guide, he was deep in conversation. He was talking about friends of his who were involved in a Baptist church. "They're more intelligent than that," he said with an air of frustration.

God's words caught in my throat. I didn't know who our guide's friends were. I didn't know what they'd said or done, if their testimony was above reproach or as human as mine. What I did know was God's children are not always popular. Of course, neither was their Messiah. But I had to honestly ask myself, *If God's truth and knowledge are on display night after night in the heavens, are they on display day after day in me?*

There's a place for theological arguments. But undoubtedly there've been times when my own flurry of spiritual rhetoric has drowned out the call of God's still, small voice. Truth and knowledge do not always need to be spoken to be heard. Just look at the northern lights.

Perhaps I need to be more like a living, breathing inukshuk, one created in the image of God, instead of the likeness of man. I should point the way toward community, warn others of danger, and remind people they're not alone in this world—without having to rely on words. After all, when it comes to creation, God considers me even more spectacular than the northern lights. If they can testify to His truth, so can I. Through me, His truth can go out into all the earth, even to the ends of the world.

> *Unspoken truth is spoken everywhere.*
> Psalm 19:4 (*The Message*)

PERSONAL JOURNEY

IF you had a free airline ticket to anywhere in the world, where would you go? What is it about this destination that stirs your heart? What does this tell you about yourself? About God at work within you?

RALPH Waldo Emerson wrote, "If the stars should appear just one night in a thousand years, how would men believe and adore!" What truth does this quote hold?

WHAT does being a living, breathing inukshuk mean to you? How do you think you are, or can be, a reminder to others that they are not alone in this world?

TRUTH is more than correct principles. Truth is part of God's character. Read John 14:6. What do you think Jesus means?

PEOPLE often disagree on what is absolute truth—or even if there is such a thing. How do you discern what is truth and what isn't? Find three verses of Scripture that help explain what truth is or how to find it. Copy them onto 3-by-5 cards. Read them, and talk to God about them, every morning for the next week.

Orvieto,

Italy

"It's dangerous in here," our guide announced with a carefree laugh. "Very dangerous." Not a spiel I'd readily heard from any tour guide in the United States. Having journeyed from the country of guardrails, safety goggles, hard hats, and lawsuits waiting to happen, I found the laxity of restrictions in some of Italy's smaller towns a refreshing change. Even so, the tour group seemed to suck in a collective breath.

"Do the streets ever cave in?" a member

The foundation of this whole city was a honeycomb of tufa— ancient, crumbling, carved-out tufa.

of our tour group asked with a hint of timidity.

"Oh yes," the guide replied, followed by another round of giggles. "Often." Still laughing, the guide pointed toward a dark staircase descending further into the labyrinth of caves below the city streets of Orvieto. "This way," she said. We seemed to have no choice but to follow. After all, we'd paid five euros.

I couldn't help but picture the cathedral I'd visited earlier in the day. The big one. Constructed with massive amounts of marble, basalt, and alabaster. Add a few hundred tourists, stone sculptures and altars, and one of the largest pipe organs in Italy. Now set it right above my head on 30-plus feet of *tufa* rock. Granite, it's not. Tufa, or tuff, is light and porous, made of volcanic residue and ash. The composite is soft, making it fairly easy to carve out the more than 1,000 rooms, tunnels, staircases, and passageways in the "underground city" beneath Orvieto. As a matter of fact, people had been doing just that since the days of the Etruscans, more than 2,500 years ago.

I never studied architecture, but I understood enough to know that the integrity of any structure was heavily dependent on its foundation. The foundation of this whole city was a honeycomb of tufa—ancient, crumbling, carved-out tufa. I tried to stop thinking about what sat above me and concentrate on proceeding down to the room below me.

I made a conscious effort to take deep, slow breaths as I entered the ink black passage. This was no time for my on-again, off-again claustrophobia to kick in. If I tried to bolt back up the stairs, I might not only bowl over some elderly tourists but possibly knock out a wall. Luckily, the staircase was so narrow turning back was hardly an option.

None too soon, the passage emptied out into a large room, complete with a "window" carved through the rock into the open air. The hole in the wall framed the picture-perfect artwork of the surrounding countryside. I scanned a leafy green patchwork of vineyards, tobacco fields, gardens, and terraces, punctuated by farmhouses, villas, an old convent, and the ever-present Italian cypress trees. The scenery looked so warm and inviting. I inhaled a deep breath of fresh air and then turned back to the dull, gray walls that surrounded me. As my eyes adjusted to the dim light, I noticed the walls were covered with a grid of small holes.

"Pigeons," our guide explained. "Many of the rooms in this underground city served as pigeon coops. Others were used for making and storing oil and wine. Still others were used for cisterns, since there was no water source on top of this rock."

And what a "rock" it was. From a distance, Orvieto looked like a storybook castle, perched on a mesa of tufa. A vertical wall rising straight up from the plains of Umbria, in some places over 3,000 feet high, formed the base of the city. It was inside this oblong wall of sheer rock cliffs that the underground city was carved.

"Do you see this staircase?" our guide continued. "Take a look! It will lead you nowhere but straight down! It empties right out the side of the cliff. That's because the soft rock has eroded away since it was built. . . ."

Great! I sighed to myself. *Erosion. Another architectural menace to contend with. . . .* As though my lunch in Civita di Bagnoregio wasn't warning enough. Yet another city—Bagnoregio—built on tufa. A few earthquakes, a couple centuries of erosion, and the far end of the city wound up being its own island in the sky. Today Civita di Bagnoregio is virtually inaccessible outside of the footbridge across the chasm between the main city of Bagnoregio and the little civita.

Nicknamed "the Dying City," Civita di Bagnoregio is home to a couple of restaurants and gift shops, as well as fewer than 25 residents. The majority of the inhabitants are elderly, spending their days sitting outside their cliff-clinging dwellings, inviting the few visitors that wander the abbreviated streets of this aerial oddity to take in the sweeping views from their gardens—for a few small coins.

Though I made it across the footbridge of Civita di Bagnoregio and later up from the tufa bowels of Orvieto's underground city without incident, I felt like I'd spent the day walking through Jesus's parable of the wise and foolish builders. Both Orvieto and Bagnoregio appeared to be built on solid rock, standing tall on what seemed a sound foundation. But closer inspection revealed that building on tufa had a lot in common with building on sand.

Is any part of my faith being undermined by tunnels of tufa instead of resting squarely on God's rock-solid foundation of truth? As I watched Orvieto's silhouette fade with the light of the setting sun from the back window of the van, I couldn't help but pose the question to myself. As for the answer, that would extend far beyond the long drive back to my hotel and my flight back over the Atlantic. It's an answer that only the course of a lifetime can reveal.

> *The man of integrity walks securely.*
> Proverbs 10:9 (NIV)

PERSONAL JOURNEY

LOOK up the word *integrity* in the dictionary. Then, write your own personal definition.

HOW is integrity essential to consistently living a life that's pleasing to God?

READ Matthew 7:24–27. (You may want to substitute the word "tufa" for "sand" as you read!) Then, ask yourself, "Is any part of my faith being undermined by tunnels of tufa, instead of resting squarely on God's rock-solid foundation of truth?"

WHAT are some other foundations, besides God's truth, that people choose to build their lives on? How are these like Orvieto's foundation?

THE integrity of Orvieto's cathedral rests on the workmanship of those who built it and the foundation that supports it. Consider your local church. How do you play a part in maintaining the integrity of its spiritual structure and foundation?

Bangkok,
Thailand

Never pat a person or a statue on the head. When seated on the floor or crossing your legs, never point the soles of your feet toward anyone. Keep a *jai yen* (a cool heart) and avoid raising your voice if there's a problem. Wear modest clothing, nothing sleeveless, and remove your sandals when entering a temple. Be aware that in place of toilet paper, you may find a hose. . . ."

After months of reading up on Thai

But the king recognized beauty where others did not.

etiquette, Buddhism, and the historical significance of the sites I would visit, I was ready to set my feet on Asian soil for the very first time. But there was one thing I wasn't quite prepared for. The culture inside our tour bus felt more foreign to me than the one outside.

That feeling first became apparent at the welcome dinner. I was the one who really didn't fit in. I was the minority, the third wheel, the odd woman out. With my husband and kids back at home, thousands of miles away, I already felt a bit out of place, unhinged, and alone. Since I was traveling with my sister and her husband, I had prepared myself to be the one searching for a seat on the bus when the rest of the group divided itself up into couples. I just didn't realize the majority of those couples would be *gay*.

By the time dinner was over, I was more than aware of the two men who stared past me as if I were invisible—or as though they wished I were. When they learned I was a Christian, from Colorado Springs, no less, it felt as though a wall of ice formed between us. The chill was evident even in the muggy evening heat. It felt like my mere presence had the power to potentially ruin their vacation. And I didn't want it to. Their presence was certainly not going to ruin mine. As a matter of fact, I felt more certain than ever that God would use this trip to expand the boundaries of my heart.

It wasn't long before I felt those borders being stretched. After dinner, our tour guide offered our group the option of going to Patpong, a district known for its sex trade, particularly underage prostitution. Although Thailand is a largely Buddhist country, and Buddhism does not condone promiscuity, Thailand has one of the most active sex trade markets in the world, accompanied by a growing epidemic of AIDS. The gay men in our group readily signed up for the "field trip." To me, it felt like kids signing up for an outing to a zoo where animals are tortured and abused. The borders of my heart did more than stretch. They broke.

I returned to my room and fell on my bed, wracked with deep-seated sobs. I couldn't stop these men from going any more than I could wipe Patpong off the map. The only thing I could think of to do was pray. So that's what I did. I prayed for the wisdom to know when to speak and when to keep silent, for the vulnerability to reach out in love, even if it wasn't returned, and for the strength to simply be myself—a flawed, yet forgiven, child of the King. Oh, and something else I prayed for was that the men going to Patpong would have a horrible time.

Early the next morning, I watched my fellow traveling companions as they boarded the bus. All of those who had gone to Patpong—except the couple behind the wall of ice—were talking about how horrible it was and how disgusted they were with what they saw. I couldn't help but smile to myself and say, *Thanks, God. I know it's a little thing, but it's a start.*

But God's answers didn't stop there. Something had changed in my own heart overnight. As we traded our bus for a boat ride down the Chao Phraya River, I found myself studying the not-yet-familiar faces around me, instead of the sites on the shore. And I was overwhelmed with compassion. The need to love and be loved was so deeply ingrained in us all. I guess that's what happens when you're created in the image of Love itself.

How we choose to fill that longing for love doesn't always follow God's design. But extending love to those around me, whether gay or straight, had nothing to do with loving, accepting, or condoning their choices. God so loved the whole world . . . a world of broken people, all originally created in His image, all who have the opportunity to become whole only because of God's transforming touch through Jesus Christ. Both saints and would-be saints had so much to teach each other about unconditional love, and therefore about God Himself. I was ready to learn. How was I to know God would use broken china as my textbook?

My mind went from reverie to reality the moment Wat Arun came into view. All of us started shifting in our seats, jockeying for position to get a good look at the temple by the water's edge. From a distance, it looked like an Empire State Building wanna-be, albeit with an Asian twist. But instead of an angular frame, the uppermost edges of the *prang* (the temple tower) were softly curved, its sides lined with vertical grooves. But as my floating vantage point changed, so did my perception. As we drew closer, the spire looked less like a skyscraper and more like a skinny wedding cake, layered tier upon willowy tier, and frosted in uniform sandstone beige.

The closer we drew to the dock, the wider my mouth opened. Uniform sandstone beige? Hardly. Wat Arun held more colors and patterns than a kaleidoscope. With both my camera and my mind's eye ready, I climbed the stairs along with the rest of the group so I could more completely comprehend what my eyes were telling me was true.

The Buddhist temple looked more like a monument to the proverbial bull in the china shop—if that bull happened to suffer from a compulsive organizational disorder. Bits and pieces of broken china, their hodgepodge patterns grouped together and then accented by brightly colored glazed tiles, formed a mosaic of fanciful flowers and intricate borders, interspersed with the fearsome faces of demons.

To say I'd never seen anything like it would be a gross understatement. The millions of shards of porcelain were donated by the Siamese people in the mid-1800s at the request of King Mongkut (of *Anna and the King* fame). The shards came from the inexpensive china used as ballast on trade ships that traveled down the Chao Phraya River from China.

It was hard to comprehend something so beautiful, so delicate—so designed for a different purpose—would be used as deadweight in the hull of empty cargo ships. This china had been originally fashioned for a place of honor at the dinner table, not ballast or rubbish. Perhaps it was its common pattern or flawed porcelain that made the china seem so insignificant at the time. Maybe it was cracked, chipped, or had shattered into pieces that seemed so damaged they could never be put together again.

But the king recognized beauty where others did not. He took what had been broken and discarded and created something entirely new, the beauty of which far surpassed what it had once been. Who would have thought such common vessels could be used for such a noble purpose?

My eyes wandered from the wonder before me to the wonders around me. In every face I saw a china pattern; and in every heart, its broken pieces. I knew my tour group would think I was nuts if they knew I was praying God would make a Wat Arun of their lives. But I knew that's exactly what He was doing with me. He'd taken every shard of my heart and made something unexpected and new. In Him I felt healed, whole, and complete. In Him I felt beautiful.

Over the next two weeks I grew in love and friendship with every member of our group. I planted seeds of faith in love and trusted God to give them growth. I even watched that "wall of ice" melt into a welcome, refreshing pool. And when the day came to say good-bye, I uttered yet another prayer. One of thanks for every person He'd brought my way in Thailand, both inside and outside the bus.

If anyone is in Christ, he is a new creation; the old has gone, the new has come!
2 Corinthians 5:17 (NIV)

PERSONAL JOURNEY

HOW do you respond when you're around people whose faith or lifestyle is very different from your own? Can you think of a recent example?

WHAT does 1 Peter 3:15 have to say about how you relate to others, especially those who may not share your faith in God? What are practical ways you can put this into practice?

READ 1 Corinthians 3:6–9. How can you play a part in someone else's journey toward becoming whole?

GOD can take what is broken and use it for His glory. In Bangkok, He took a temple built to honor Buddhism and used it to lead me to a place of insight, worship, and praise. How is God making a Wat Arun of your life?

REWRITE 2 Corinthians 5:17 in your own words, thanking God for the "old brokenness" that has gone and the "new wholeness" that has come.

Armstrong Grove,

California

Buckling myself into the seat of a plane had always been an opportunity for joy. Nonexistent legroom, unpredictable turbulence, lilliputian-sized snacks . . . they never fazed me. They were just part of the journey, my penance for privilege, a precursor to untold adventure. But today there was no trace of joy. No trace of anything, for that matter. I felt hollow, vacant, so emotionally untethered that a gusty spring breeze could pick me up, lift

Occasionally, a ray of sunlight pierced the dense roof of branches above, spotlighting tiny, delicate plant life on the forest floor.

me high into the clouds, and I wouldn't even feel the rush of flight. I knew God was still there, but I certainly didn't feel His touch. I didn't feel anything.

I glanced at my fellow passengers. I wondered how many of them were in the same place I was. How many were not traveling for pleasure or business? How many were heading to a destination they dreaded? A funeral. A court proceeding. A risky medical procedure. Or perhaps, like me, to a hospital room to stand beside someone they loved.

When the call came in the middle of the night several days before, I'd let it ring. *Probably a wrong number,* I reasoned. I was already emotionally spent. That evening I'd helped plan a funeral for a friend. Looking through old photos, talking through verses of Scripture, choosing favorite songs, reminiscing about years gone by . . . it felt like we were planning a party for Pam, instead of a memorial service. But the guest of honor had gone on ahead of us to her new home in view of God's throne. I felt like we were the "uninvited." Her family and friends were the ones left behind to clean up the confetti and limp balloons, the tokens of a life well lived.

The ringing phone went silent. I relaxed and tried to go back to sleep. Not more than 30 seconds passed before the ringing started right up again. Something was wrong. Now fully awake, I headed down to the kitchen to pick up the phone. My sister was on the other end.

"Mom's had a stroke. . . . Dad was out of town. . . . They don't know how long she was lying there. . . . I'm flying out in the morning. . . ."

Soon I was on a plane as well. As my flight began its descent into San Francisco, I watched curls of fog wrap themselves around the hills of the Bay Area. I craned my neck to look toward Oakland, the city where I'd been born, then at Richmond and El Cerrito where I'd spent my elementary school years. On those hills I'd built tree forts, learned to read, and broken my arm attempting to roller-skate down the middle of a nearly vertical neighborhood street. On those hills I'd watched my mother cook, clean, work for my father's company, and entertain hoards of dinner guests. On those hills, my grandparents were buried. And someday, I surmised, my mother would be buried there too. But not today.

Today she was lying in a coma in a hospital in Santa Rosa. The prognosis was uncertain. So we sat, my sister, my brother-in-law, and I. We spoke in whispers, moved in slow motion, repeatedly scanned the sheets over my mother's frail frame for the slightest movement . . . the twitch of a toe, the bending of a finger, the flutter of an eyelid. But all we saw was the rise and fall of my mother's chest, aided by the breathing tube snaked down her throat.

As the days passed, Cindy, Lee, and I slipped into "comas" of our own. We lost touch with life beyond sterile floors, cafeteria food, and the sympathetic smiles of the hospital staff. All we could do was sit, watch, wait, and pray. But my prayers felt as shallow as my mother's breath. *If my mother will be able to draw closer to You, to still find joy in life, then please, Lord, bring her back. If not* . . . I never quite knew where to go from there.

"We've got to get out of here for a while," my sister whispered one morning. "Let's drive out to the coast and back through Armstrong Grove. The hospital can reach us by cell phone if there's any change."

I felt a surge of joy, immediately followed by a knockout punch of guilt. I was all too eager to trade these four walls for the promise of adventure, to put aside my bedside vigil for my own pleasure, to do what my mother could not—to leave. But it was more than just my suffocating spirit calling me out into the fresh air. There was something more. God's whisper was calling out from somewhere deep within me. *Come on. It's OK. I'm waiting for you* . . .

That's when I knew. I had a date with God in the redwoods. He was waiting for me beneath the forest canopy of Armstrong Grove. It sounded as weird to me then as it does now, but that doesn't make it any less true. I knew the presence of God was as close to me by my mother's bedside as He would be beside the sea, among the trees, or around the world. After all, that's what *omni*presence is all about. And yet, there was something special waiting for me beneath the redwood trees. I was certain. Everything within me perked up in expectation. I awoke from my coma and climbed into the backseat of the car.

We wound our way along back roads to the coast, leisured over steaming bowls of clam chowder and spongy bricks of sourdough bread spread with a layer of butter as thick as mortar. We watched seabirds and sea lions, scavenged shells, and felt our shoes grow heavy with sand as we walked along the fog-laden shore. I savored every minute, but felt certain something even sweeter awaited me.

As we drove along the Russian River the sun burned through the fog revealing pools of turquoise sky. I looked up and looked back. So many years had passed since I'd traveled this road. A school field trip or a Camp Fire Girls campout, I couldn't recall which, was the last time I'd walked beneath the giant sequoias. In the life span of a redwood my last 30 years was little more than the blink of an eye. I knew the trees of Armstrong Grove would be a little taller, a little broader; but from a human perspective they'd be virtually unchanged. As for me, in 30 years more had changed than remained the same.

But the sight of the redwoods brought out the little girl in me. As we pulled into the parking lot my heart gave a silent cry, "Daddy! I'm home!" I jumped out of the car with all the exuberance of my Camp Fire Girls days. Beneath my feet lay a downy cushion of cinnamon-colored bark. Above me massive branches blocked the brilliant sky from view. I took off up a nearby trail. In a matter of minutes I left Cindy and Lee far behind.

I sent bursts of praise, worship, and wonder skyward. God rained showers of encouragement, comfort, and joy down in return. I ran my fingers along the soft crags of feathered bark, kicked up clouds of redwood "fuzz," and breathed in air infused with the scent of soil and redwood mulch bathed in the last drops of morning dew.

Occasionally, a ray of sunlight pierced the dense roof of branches above, spotlighting tiny, delicate plant life on the forest floor. Like me, they were surrounded by giants, trees that had stood 500, 1,000, almost 1,500 years. The sequoias towered above me, rising higher than Coit Tower in San Francisco. Two hundred to 300 feet tall, the redwoods in this grove would dwarf a blue whale, which is so often referred to as the world's largest living thing. It would take two to three whales balanced tail-to-tail to rise as high as the "living things" that surrounded me.

The mental picture of acrobatic whales made me smile. It was good to know I hadn't forgotten how.

I bent backward, eyes to the treetops. I was so small next to such grandeur. But while I felt miniscule in size, I knew God saw me as mightier than a redwood. My life on earth would be shorter than that of the grove that surrounded me, but in God's grand scheme of time these trees would be the creation that disappeared in the blink of an eye. I would be the one that remained, my roots growing deep, my branches spreading wide in worship throughout eternity.

In that moment, in that place, I felt embraced, sheltered, wholly at home. God's presence was as close as my own breath. But why? Why was He so near to me here yet so far away on the plane? Was experiencing His presence a gift? A fluke? A figment of my own desperate heart? God said He'd be "close to those whose hearts are breaking," but did that mean the heartbroken would be more aware of His presence? God was always near, whether or not I heard His whisper, whether or not I felt His touch.

I thought of my mother, lying motionless beneath starched white sheets. For years we'd lived in different states and traveled to other countries. Throughout my adult life, there'd surely been days when my mother didn't even come to mind. When she wasn't physically present, was my mother's "presence" in my life diminished? Did I love her any less? Did the reality of our relationship come into question? Of course not.

My relationship with God was different. There was no physical presence to draw near to, no image to keep in a frame by my bedside, no tangible hand to hold in times of trouble. But God was there, as close as a mother's love, as solid as a Father's promises. His presence remained with me, whether I felt Him or not, the day my mother opened her eyes, the day she relearned to talk, to walk, to eat, to dream.

I know that one day my mother will return to the hills by the Bay for the very last time. When that day comes, I'm certain God's presence will remain as close to me as my own breath. And when I've exhaled the last of this life, God's presence will still be by my side. Only this time I'll get to see Him face-to-face.

> *The Lord is close to those whose hearts are breaking.*
> Psalm 34:18 (TLB)

PERSONAL JOURNEY

IS it easier for you to believe God is near when you feel some hint of His presence? Why or why not?

HOW have you experienced the presence of God? What was going on emotionally, physically, and/or spiritually in your life at the time?

ON occasion in the Old Testament, God would manifest Himself in a physical way. Why do you think this isn't the "norm" today?

READ Psalm 89:15–17. What characteristics do those who "walk in the light" of God's presence display? When are these characteristics most evident in you?

DOES your heart feel broken today? If so, draw close to the One who promises to draw close to you. Picture yourself handing every shard of your shattered heart over to Him. Surrender your hurt to Him. Allow Him to heal your heart in His time, in His way.

T here are only two reasons I would attend a sporting event. My children's participation or if attendance included a free ticket to France. Considering that neither of my children have a competitive team sport bone in their bodies—a blessing for which I am eternally grateful—I was sitting on a hard wooden bench in well-below-freezing weather staring at a small oblong of ice, but in the shadow of the French Alps. My

I was cheering him on like a wild woman.

mother sat beside me, bundled up in more layers than a croissant at a pâtisserie.

The Winter Olympics was one of my mother's personal passions. Every 4 years for the last 16, she'd invited a friend to accompany her to the games. She'd taken her mother to Lake Placid, a friend to Sarajevo, and my sister to Calgary. Now it was my turn to journey with her to Albertville, France.

However, the "wide world of sports" was one world I'd never cared to explore. I tried to be interested once. A dear friend had an intense passion for football. To try to understand her heart on a deeper level, I decided to actually join her in watching a game. After all, I lived in Colorado and the Broncos were a team I'd heard was worth rooting for. So I gave it a shot. I joined a group of friends at her house and sat down to watch the game on TV.

Frankly, I was bored. Men ran back and forth with a ball, tried to knock it out of each other's hands, and then threw themselves on each other in a big pile. I'd seen this behavior a thousand times before when I'd raised toddlers. For this, grown men made millions of dollars? I was at a loss. But then the sun broke through the clouds over the field. For a moment I was absolutely enchanted.

"You know," I said over the shouting and hooting going on all around me, "If you follow the shadows on the field, it looks like they're dancing."

The commotion in the room came to a screeching halt. I felt as if I'd just uttered a curse word during a sermon. So ended my attempt to become a sports fan.

But here I was sitting on the sidelines, preparing to cheer. For the first time in Olympic history, short-track speed skating was about to make its debut as a medal sport. Of course, individual sports were easier for me to connect with than team sports. I didn't really care about scores and goals and supporting a team by wearing a wedge of cheese on my head. But I did care about individuals striving to do their best with the gifts and abilities God gave them. I guess it was just easier for me to connect with athletes when they didn't come in a pack.

One of those athletes was Dan Jansen. Here was a speed skater with numerous world records and world cups to his name. But at this point he seemed more famous for what he hadn't done. He hadn't won Olympic gold, or any Olympic medal for that matter. Four years ago his sister had died of leukemia during the Olympic Games, on the morning of his 500-meter race. During the race, Jansen fell and slid off the track. The chance for a medal slipped away in the 1,000-meter race as well.

Four years had passed and Jansen was back. And I was there to see him. OK, to root for him. Who wouldn't? This didn't feel like "sports." This felt like life. Here was someone who refused to give up, who persevered through failure and heartache. Here was someone I actually wanted to see win. If the concession booth had sold foam speed skates to wear on our heads with *Go, Dan!* stamped on them, I probably would have sprung for one.

The people next to us seemed even more excited to see Jansen skate than we were. Little wonder. As we struck up a conversation with the parka-clad guy to our right, we discovered we were seated in the midst of Jansen's most passionate fan club—his family. Brother-in-law, cousin-of-a-cousin twice-removed, or whoever this relative was, he gave my mother and me a running commentary as Jansen readied himself at the starting line. All conversation came to a halt as we awaited the sound of the starting pistol.

Then I did something I never dreamed I'd do in any way, shape, or form having to do with sports. I prayed. It was short, simple, and to the point. I simply asked God to help Dan concentrate and do his best.

One loud crack and skates started flying, arms started pumping, and fans started screaming. "Oh no," the man next to us moaned. "Look at his hands! He's lost it." In that split second, even before the skaters had rounded the first turn, the guy next to us knew the outcome.

It was all over just 37 seconds after it had begun. I couldn't believe it. It was over? That was it? People trained years, hour upon hour, week after week for 37 seconds? Surely this had to be just a warm-up round or something!

But those 37 seconds were the real thing. According to our personal commentator, Jansen didn't have his hands in the right position when the starting pistol went off and that error cost him a medal. He finished ½ second behind first place and ²/₁₀ second behind third. Little more than the blink of an eye. But in speed skating, the blink of an eye, or apparently the position of a hand, could mean the difference between winning and losing. Jansen's family packed up their American flags and headed down to the track. My mom and I headed back to our hotel.

"Thirty-seven seconds," I kept repeating to my mom. "Could you devote your whole life to train for something that lasted 37 seconds?"

I doubted I could. It was tough enough for me to devote myself completely to things that would last for eternity, things like purity, righteousness, and love. When it came to my faith, what kind of athlete was I? How well did I persevere when I blew it and "slipped on the track"? When the competition got tough? When I faced personal heartache? When I was tired, discouraged, or in pain?

The truth is, like Dan Jansen, I was ultimately in a race against myself. He and I faced some of the same obstacles: Can I put the past behind me? Can I beat my personal best? Can I put everything I know into practice, focusing solely on what I need to do? Can I persevere no matter what—or will I choose to quit?

Dan Jansen didn't take home a medal from either of his two races in Albertville. Two years later, in Lillehammer, Norway, Jansen slipped in the 500-meter race and came in eighth. Later, in the 1,000, he slipped again. But this time he went on to win the gold. I'll never forget the image of him holding his baby daughter in his arms as he took his victory lap around the track.

From the couch in my family room, I was cheering him on like a wild woman. If my family hadn't known better, they would have thought they were in the presence of a sports fan. When I finally cross life's finish line, I'd sure love to see God cheer like that for me.

> *You've all been to the stadium and seen the athletes race. Everyone runs; one wins. Run to win. All good athletes train hard. They do it for a gold medal that tarnishes and fades. You're after one that's gold eternally.*
> 1 Corinthians 9:24–25 (*The Message*)

PERSONAL JOURNEY

DO you have a favorite athlete? If so, what makes him or her worth admiring?

IF your salvation depends solely on what Christ did, not what you do, why does it matter if you persevere?

WHAT kind of athlete are you when it comes to your faith? What is your biggest stumbling block in terms of perseverance?

FINISH the passage of Scripture at the end of the chapter by reading 1 Corinthians 9:26–27. What part does self-discipline and keeping focused on God play in perseverance?

READ the parable of the talents in Matthew 25:14–30. Then, picture God welcoming you into heaven with the words of the master, "Well done, good and faithful servant!" How would that compare to winning a gold medal? Spend a few moments in prayer talking with your Father about that future day.

The Golden Triangle,

Asia

My husband was on the other side of the world. I knew he'd never approve, but I was desperate. I opened the door then shut it again. I shouldn't. Rationalization ran rampant through my brain. . . . *I spent the entire morning riding in the back of a pickup truck, breathing exhaust fumes, and bouncing over mountain roads. Now, it's so muggy my clothes are sticking to me like grease on a griddle. I finally have a few minutes to relax and all I really want . . .*

We may have looked different on the outside, but our feminine insecurities could have made us twins.

I opened the door again. I grabbed the ice-cold soft drink out of the minibar and popped the lid. I drank. And it was good. I figured that Mark, my über budget-conscious husband, would never have to know.

Of course, if I'd realized at that moment what I discovered at checkout time—that my minibar extravagance cost all of 60 cents—I'd have been tempted to spring for seconds. And if Mark had been there with me, he might even have joined me in a toast.

Despite the heat and humidity, I plopped myself on the rattan chair on the balcony and sipped my cola as if it were a fine wine, enjoying both the refreshment and the view. The milky brown Mekong River flowed right past my hotel. Over the river to my right was Laos. Dead ahead of me lay the border of Myanmar, which in my mind would always remain Burma. I sat in Thailand, the third corner of the famed Golden Triangle.

The name sounded so exotic, so enticing, so lyrical—until I learned the Golden Triangle earned its title from the thriving opium trade that had brought wealth to this region since the late 1800s. Opium production in Thailand dropped by more than 80 percent after it was made illegal in 1959, but the demand persisted. That meant the Golden Triangle still had an incentive to live up to its name.

People and their addictions . . . I thought with a wince of guilt, eyeing the can in my hand. As I took a final—now lukewarm—sip, I headed back inside to change. It was time to venture across the Friendship Bridge.

But the bridge that links Sop Ruak, Thailand, with Tachilek, Myanmar, is not always friendly. The Burmese government is known as both oppressive and fickle and can restrict foreigners' entry into the country at a moment's notice. As our small group of travelers walked onto the bridge, I felt the warmth and welcome of the Thai culture fade behind us. Our group's usual banter and laughter took a more hushed, guarded tone. The presence of military uniforms intimidated me, sending my usually inquisitive eyes down to survey my shoes.

As I entered the checkpoint office, I glanced up long enough to meet the glance of a distinguished Burmese officer. Every strand of his silver-flecked hair lay in perfect order along the band of his khaki government cap. In between barking orders, he was unpeeling the small, russet husks that hung from a branch of longan fruit. The moist, milky-colored fruit inside reminded me of an eyeball. Not something I readily wanted to pop into my mouth. But the officer stopped barking orders, gave me a warm smile, and offered me the gift of a small bunch of fruit. It was my olive branch from the country of Burma. What could I do but smile and accept?

I extended a thank-you in both English and Thai. I didn't know one syllable of Burmese. Our necessary visas went through in a matter of minutes. Somehow the stranger's spontaneous gift helped draw my eyes back upward. Visa now in hand, as well as my branch of longan fruit, I climbed into the rock-hard seat of a rickshaw. The driver took off like a Burmese bat out of you-know-where.

Clinging tightly to the sides of the rickshaw, I tried to take in every possible detail of the surroundings as they flew by. It was hard to believe Tachilek was just a two-minute walk across a bridge from Thailand. The northern border towns of Thailand were not affluent by any stretch of my imagination, but the seedy streets I was currently careening through made them feel as though they deserved a 90210 ZIP Code.

The trickle of a river flowing through town held more trash than water. The streets followed suit. People's clothing—as well as their expressions—seemed worn, frayed, ill-fitting. Some stared at our group while others would not meet our eye. Children, grime caked under their fingernails and over their faces, held out empty hands for coins. A young boy wearing camouflage fatigues and wielding a (hopefully) toy gun, followed our group crying out something in a language we had no way to understand. At the open-air market, unidentifiable cuts of meat curled in the afternoon sun, flies clinging to every reeking surface. Shop stalls held a conglomeration of faded rock band T-shirts, Michael Jordan posters, and Osama bin Laden backpacks and lunchboxes.

My heart and mind tried to take in the reality of the life that was being lived all around me. When I had the chance to walk through the market on my own, I focused in on individual faces, praying for each and every one that caught my eye. The women's faces were painted with swirls of white and gold powder, both to protect them from the sun and to make their complexion look more like mine—pale, white.

Our guide had explained to us earlier how white skin and a pointed nose were regarded as beautiful in this part of the world. And here I was wishing I could trade in my big nose and freckled complexion for the delicate features, golden mocha-toned skin, and impossibly small hips of the diminutive women who surrounded me. We may have looked different on the outside, but our feminine insecurities could have made us twins.

In the crush of the market crowd, I caught sight of a young mother so strikingly beautiful I couldn't help but stare. Her cheeks were adorned with ivory curlicues. She held a baby whose smile made me long to reach out and give her a squeeze. I caught the woman's eye across the continual flow of people, held up my camera, and motioned to ask permission to take a photo of her and her child. With a shy smile she nodded and posed the baby proudly on her hip.

Time after time I raised my camera, but a flood of people would pass between us, blocking my shot. Patiently, the woman continued to stand, wait, and smile. When I was finally able to snap a photo, the stranger gave me a grin as warm as any I'd received from a close friend and then continued on her way.

As I do so often when I travel, my mind played "what if?" "What if I'd been given her life instead of mine? How would I view God? How would I view the world? How would I view myself and those around me?" I'd asked myself the same questions the evening before when I'd visited the Laotian corner of the Golden Triangle.

Shortly before the sun set I'd taken a long-tail boat ride from the Thai side of the Mekong to the island of Don Sao in Laos. An assortment of cracked and discolored life jackets hung above me from the flimsy roof of the boat silently announcing, "If this boat flips, you'd better be a strong swimmer!"

When we docked, I found Don Sao was little more than a patch of souvenir stands on an almost deserted shore. I wandered past a dusty assortment of T-shirts and textiles, bottles of "snake" whiskey, and a few wild monkeys. In the end it was the boat ride itself that yielded the greatest treasure. Amidst clumps of kapok trees, I saw families gathered together in the murky currents of the Mekong. Here they washed pots and pans, dirty clothes, and themselves. As the daylight grew dim, I didn't see a single electric lightbulb or headlight illuminate the Laotian shoreline.

Across the river, just a short boat ride away, I surveyed the banks of Thailand and Burma. Though easily within view of those enjoying their evening bath, both countries were off-limits to the people of Laos. Every evening, the people of Don Sao could view the bright lights of Burma's casino, tempting tourists from across the Thai border to indulge in a guilty pleasure not available in their predominantly Buddhist country. The Laotian people could also take in the brightly lit streets of Thailand's Sop Ruak, bustling with vendors, tourists, and automobiles.

To me, the Golden Triangle seemed more like a Golden Noose, dangling the haves in front of the have-nots day after day. So close in proximity, yet so far from each other in lifestyle, governmental freedoms, and wealth. And then there was me, the tourist from halfway around the world. Wasn't I doing the same? Didn't the cash in my wallet, my fancy camera, and the very fact that I could afford to travel so far to witness people with so little light me up like a billboard that read, *Here's someone who's rich beyond your wildest dreams?*

It didn't matter that my own country labeled me middle class. In much of the world anyone who could spend 60 cents on a soda without batting an eye would be considered living a life of privilege. Of course, whether I happened to be a have or a have-not didn't matter to God. What He was more concerned with was whether I longed to have— or be—what I wasn't. Whether I'd covet the lifestyles of others or be content with the life He'd set before me. Whether what I saw would lead me on a journey toward gratitude, compassion, and contentment—or whether I'd firmly plant my feet on a self-centered path of indifference.

I returned to my hotel with the cool breeze of twilight. Walking back out onto my balcony, I watched lights click on in neighboring hotel rooms and patrons gather beneath glowing lanterns for the feast of yet another Thai dinner buffet. I looked toward Laos. The flames of a single fire were a pinprick of light on the shadowed shore. And off in the distance, the lights of Burma's casino would burn all night.

As I breathed in the sultry scent of the white angel's trumpet blooming nearby, a wave of compassion for those around me, as well as contentment with my own life washed over me. Was that contentment born more easily out of plenty than want? Undoubtedly. I was living a life that was rich beyond my own wildest dreams.

Yet the core of what I felt had nothing to do with the balance in my bank account or even the lavish blessings I'd been granted in life. Mine was the simple joy of being who I am, a child of the Great I Am. At that moment, the Golden Triangle offered me a golden opportunity. My prayers and praise flowed as freely as the waters of the Mekong.

> *I have learned the secret of being content in any and every situation, whether well fed or hungry, whether living in plenty or in want.*
> Philippians 4:12 (NIV)

PERSONAL JOURNEY

IN what area of your life do you struggle the most with being content? Finances? Personal appearance? Employment opportunities? Possessions? Or . . .?

READ 1 Timothy 6:6–8. How content are you with food and clothing? Is shopping or eating to excess ever a struggle for you? If so, why—what are you in "need" of?

IN Philippians 4, Paul talks about having been through times of need and times of abundance. Have you experienced both? What has God taught you through your experiences?

WHY would your contentment, or lack thereof, matter to God?

DO you think there's a benefit to visiting a part of the world where people live a more meager existence than you do? Why or why not?

Journey Toward . . .

PRAYER

Turkey,
Almost . . .

W ith every turn of the globe, my tears flowed. Feeling self-conscious and on the verge of blubbering aloud, I glanced at my husband. Eyes closed, singing with abandon, lost in worship . . . he certainly wouldn't notice the potential breakdown happening to his right. Chances are neither would the rest of those singing songs of praise around me.

Good. I'd grown rather accustomed to

Today nothing mattered more than those who'd lost their lives and the loved ones they'd left behind.

my dissolving into tears at the drop of a prayer request, but this seemed a little over the top even for me. If only I could find some tissues buried in the bottom of my purse . . . Nothing. A big sniff would have to suffice.

I glanced back up toward the front of the room. An enormous globe of the world revolved slowly in front of a picture window framing a view of the Rocky Mountains. Once more, the "earth's" revolution revealed the borders of Turkey. In response, my emotional floodgates let loose another tidal wave.

I pictured faces and places. People I'd met only in my prayers. Cities I'd seen only in photos. In less than three weeks I'd journey to the country represented on the globe. But apparently my heart had already set sail.

"Why would anyone want to go to Turkey?" a co-worker had asked Mark earlier in the week. When my husband casually relayed the comment to me over dinner a few nights before, it opened yet another floodgate—of words.

"Hasn't he heard of Ephesus? Paul? The Book of Ephesians? How about Mount Ararat, you know, where Moses supposedly docked the ark? And the city of Troy—the one with the big horse? How about Cappadocia and all those underground cities and churches where Christians hid from the Romans? Istanbul? Whirling dervishes? Turkish delight? And don't get me started on Pergamum and the Hittites," I ranted.

"Too late," my husband said with a knowing smile. Actually, he never said those two words aloud, but I knew what that smile meant. I'd seen that look countless times before. Almost 20 years of marriage had more than clued Mark into my passion for personal exploration of places I'd previously traveled only by book. And this time, in Turkey, Mark would be by my side. That in itself felt like a minor miracle.

My husband and I measure travel on different scales. For me, the farther outside my comfort zone and previous experience a destination is, the more I long to go. Mark considers any place lacking a sparkling-clean Western-style toilet and a McDonald's "Third World." A place to read about in the news, pray about at church, and support through missions, but certainly not consider as a potential vacation destination.

When I asked Mark if he could journey to anywhere in the world, where would he choose to go, he replied, "Epcot Center at Disney World! That way I could visit lots of different countries, but everyone would speak English and I wouldn't get sick eating the food." He didn't mention the availability of clean restrooms, but I knew that was a given.

So when Mark said yes to an opportunity to travel to Turkey with me, I was overjoyed. I knew it wasn't at the top of his "to-see" list. But I also knew sharing my passion with the guy I am most passionate about would make both of our journeys more complete. For months I read travel guides and history books, giving my ever-patient husband minilectures on everything I learned. I wanted Mark to be as excited about the trip as I was, for his soul to hunger for a connection with Turkey and its people.

My hunger was already insatiable. I poured over our itinerary, calculated how many hours we'd spend per day on the bus, and studied maps of the terrain. I listened to Turkish language tapes in the car. I wanted to at least be able to bid my newfound Turkish friends hello and good-bye. After weeks of work I also could count successfully to ten. I was ready. Mentally and emotionally, my bags were packed.

No wonder my heart was so tender toward the people of Turkey that night at the worship service. They were family I had adopted into my heart. All that was left to do was meet them in person. But I never got the chance.

A few days later, the world stopped turning. At least, it felt like it did. The Twin Towers in New York City were turned to rubble and dust. The Pentagon crumbled. Heroes disguised as ordinary men and women took a stand over a field in rural Pennsylvania. America wept. And the world joined in.

I sat in front of the TV—silent—a witness to the unthinkable. I watched news footage of papers falling from the sky like a flurry of snowflakes. Yesterday they must have all seemed so important: contracts and memos, bottom lines and big deals, timelines and to-do lists. Today nothing mattered more than those who'd lost their lives and the loved ones they'd left behind.

"So are you still going to Turkey?" a friend asked on the phone that evening.

"Why wouldn't I?" I replied.

"Well, they're Muslim there, right?" she said. "I couldn't imagine getting on a plane and flying anywhere right now, least of all to an Islamic country."

I could. I could still picture the country in my mind, long for it in my heart. Turkey was not Afghanistan. Turkey does share borders with Syria, Iran, and Iraq; I wasn't planning on trekking through potential war zones. As for the primary religion of Turkey being Islam, the nightly news showed how people were lashing out at Muslims here in the US. That made me long to travel to Turkey even more, to be a flesh-and-blood follower of Christ who could reach out with compassion to individuals created in God's image, regardless of where they were at this moment on their own spiritual journey. I wanted to bathe the country in prayer, to press my hand against the tour bus window and call upon God's blessing and revelation to spill out onto the countryside as it passed by.

And I did—but not from a bouncing bus seat. In the wake of upheaval and uncertainty, our trip was canceled. But that didn't mean I couldn't journey to Turkey. Instead of by plane, I traveled via prayer.

Through my "almost" trip to Turkey, I discovered prayer is a marvelous way to travel for the most, to the least, intrepid adventurer. There's no language barrier, no jet lag, and even clean restrooms (as long as I keep up on my housekeeping). Almost every day I make an unscheduled journey to somewhere, as I pray my way through the morning news.

I may never see firsthand the shores of the Aegean coast, walk the same streets Paul once did in the city of Ephesus, or bid "merhaba" to a newfound Turkish friend, but I can travel to Turkey and beyond every day of my life. I can touch people around the world in the way my heart longs to do. I can make a difference in the world. I can pray.

> *My house will be called a house of prayer for all nations.*
> Isaiah 56:7 (NIV)

PERSONAL JOURNEY

WHAT did you know about the country of Turkey before you read this chapter? How does understanding more about a foreign nation strengthen your compassion for its people?

DO you believe it's important to pray regularly for other nations around the world? If so, how do you respond to this need?

THIS week, encourage a missionary working in a foreign country by writing him or her a letter or sending an email. Seal it with prayer.

REVELATION 5:8 describes the prayers of God's children as "incense" in heaven. Talk to God in prayer about prayer. What is your typical prayertime like? Is there any way you'd like to see that time change?

CHOOSE one country in the world you know little about. Over the next month, journey there via travel guides, history books, and/or information on the Internet. Spend a few minutes each day praying specifically for this nation. At the end of the month, gauge what God has done in your own heart toward this country and its people. You may have to wait until heaven to know what your prayers have brought about in this part of the world.

Journey Toward . . .
STRENGTH

Somewhere in the Amazon

I turned the travel brochure over. On the back flap was a picture of a naked man. The fellow did have a string around his waist and a spear in his hand, but other than that he was as unencumbered as Adam on his very first day.

"That's where we're going to end up," I said to Cherie, pointing to Mr. Au Naturel. "A survival camp."

"Don't be ridiculous," she replied. "We're going to one of those places where

"This wasn't on the itinerary," I muttered to Cherie. To God, I said nothing.

you watch birds from rope bridges in trees and lounge in hammocks with an umbrella in your drink."

I so wished I didn't have to say, "I told you so." But I did. There'd be no umbrellas in our drinks. But there would be rice served with monkey meat in our lunch. Still there was something to be thankful for. Our guide was wearing more than dental floss.

I do enjoy the outdoors. But for me, the outdoors has its limits. I don't sleep in the wild without a tent. I don't make friends with unfriendly wildlife. I don't hunt. I don't fish. And I don't clean anything hunters or fisherman bring home for supper. That is, I didn't, until my friend and I were bumped from our overbooked cushy lodge on the Amazon River and wound up here. Wherever "here" was. All I knew was that the city of Iquitos lay several hours behind us by speedboat and that my blow dryer was going to need a much longer cord to connect with electricity of any kind.

Our guide Llaco ([Yakko]; pronounced like one of the characters on the *Animaniacs*) showed me, Cherie, and a Japanese gentleman loaded down with some very expensive looking fishing gear, around our new home away from home. First Llaco led us to the bathrooms. Rustic, but adequate. Next he showed us our "lodge." Three cots draped in mosquito netting sat in the middle of a weather-beaten wooden platform covered by a tin roof. "This is where the girls will sleep," Llaco said. I immediately felt as if I were on a sleepover back in junior high. "Men over here." Llaco pointed the master fisherman, who didn't speak any English, down a walkway a bit further into the jungle. Tour complete.

"Get settled and then come down to the river for a boat ride," Llaco called back as he left. I tossed my suitcase under a cot. Settled. I grabbed my camera and headed for the dock—or should I say the steps made of tree branches lodged into the slippery bank that led down to the sewer-brown water. Noting my arrival, Llaco cautioned, "You'd better leave that camera here. You wouldn't want it to fall in the water if the boat tips over."

That's when I noticed the speedboat was gone. The only

transportation that remained was a dugout canoe. It was more than "rough-hewn." It was tilted, leaking, and already sitting pretty low in the water. Wait until we plopped four people stuffed with monkey into it. I took my camera to higher ground. Too bad Llaco didn't give me the option of staying to guard it.

As I headed back down toward the water's edge, I took note: four people, three seats. "Not a problem," Llaco said offhandedly. Well, not for Llaco, Cherie, or the master fisherman. They each got one of the official plank seats. Llaco tossed me a postcard-sized plank of wood and a plastic saucer.

"Just wedge that wood near the middle of the canoe," Llaco instructed. "And when the water reaches your ankles, use the saucer to bail."

I looked Llaco straight in the eye. He was serious. So was I.

From all outside appearances, I probably seemed to be pretty good-natured about the whole thing. But inside, there was a war of words going on and God was getting an earful.

OK, God, I've been a good sport so far, but this was NOT on the itinerary! I'm going to breathe too hard, tip this canoe, and send us all into the stinky depths of this brown cesspool where we'll be torn apart by rabid piranha. This is NOT the way I want to go! My family won't even be able to locate my body. I can't even locate me! I want my hammock! I want my umbrella drink! I want to go home . . .

The only response I heard was the cry of some unknown bird in the jungle canopy. If I'd been at the other lodge I could be viewing that bird from a rope bridge with a wildlife identification book in one hand and, of course, my exotic fruit juice beverage in the other. Instead, I felt something tickling my ankles. I started bailing as we started heading downriver. So much for dry sneakers.

Llaco stopped his commentary about the jungle flora and fauna midsentence. I froze. What fresh danger faced us now? There was murmuring, mumbling. The noise sounded like a group of old women gossiping discretely behind raised, wrinkled hands. And the sound was coming from under our canoe.

I peered into the water, trying ever so hard not to rock the boat; but I couldn't see anything through the murky cocoa in which we were floating. "Talking catfish," Llaco explained. I felt like I'd walked into an episode of *The X-Files*.

OK, God, this is kind of cool. Talking catfish! Who knew? What will You think up next . . .?

God knows I'm such a pushover. A little mystery, a little wonder, and I'm hooked. Suddenly, I no longer wanted to head home. I wondered what else He had on the itinerary.

"Anybody up for a little piranha fishing?" Llaco asked.

OK, God, You almost had me. I take it back. I want to go home. . . .

The master fisherman was all smiles. He carefully selected one of his shiny new rods, baited the hook, and adeptly sent the line sailing over the surface of the water. Llaco handed me a stick with a string. I knew *Candid Camera* must be hiding somewhere nearby.

Fishing had never been on my list of things I'd like to try. Something about skewering one slimy thing to try to catch another while spending copious amounts of time sitting and staring never rang my fun button. But what else could I do? Llaco was already attaching some funky-looking bug to my hook. Its life was almost over. The least I could do was not let it die in vain. I dropped the string over the side of the canoe.

Almost instantly the string began to dance. I felt a surge of adrenaline. "Hey!" I yelled to Llaco. The master fisherman looked pale.

But now I faced another dilemma. How do you reel in a string? I yanked the pole up into the air and back toward the boat, sending an angry, thrashing piranha sailing through the sky—and directly into Llaco's face. Between the wildly swaying canoe; the flying, flapping fish; and our surprised guide trying to regain his composure, chaos reigned momentarily. But Llaco was a pro. He unhooked the still active piranha, its pointy little teeth clacking away, and unceremoniously tossed it into the bottom of the boat. With me.

Again, dilemma. I contemplated how I'd explain to my doctor how I'd received such an unusual injury in such a delicate spot.

But almost instantaneously, my anxiety was replaced by wonder. The piranha, which seconds before had been ruby red-flecked with shining silver had quickly turned a flat, matte gray. It lay lifeless below me looking like any garden variety fish at the grocer's seafood counter. Well, any ordinary fish sporting a set of Dracula fangs.

OK, God, You got me again. . . .

For the next hour or so we baited, waited, and then pulled in piranha ranging in color from red to orange to silver. Then we watched them fade to gray. As the sun began to set, the final count was five for me, three each for Cherie and Llaco. And for the master fisherman? Zip.

As we rowed against the current toward "home," I hoped against hope that a Marriott had been built in our absence. My feet were wet, my arms were tired, the humidity was stifling, and dead fish were beginning to bob around the bottom of the boat as the water rose yet again to my ankles. My spirit of adventure was waning. As if on cue, God turned on the mood lighting. The Amazon looked like Fifth Avenue on Christmas Day. Clouds of fireflies filled the branches of the trees on the riverbank for as far as I could see.

I was glad it was dark. I didn't want anyone to see the tears that wet my cheeks. The rest of the group might think I wanted to go home. On the contrary, God's unparalleled creativity had simply reduced me to a puddle of awe.

Lord, this is only the first day! What else can You possibly have ahead for me . . .?

"Tomorrow is the day you've all been looking forward to," Llaco began as we secured the canoe near camp. "Tomorrow we'll head deep into the jungle with only mosquito netting, rope, and a knife. We'll each spend time alone, eating only what we can catch."

At this point, Jekyll and Hyde had nothing on me. "This wasn't on the itinerary," I muttered to Cherie. To God, I said nothing. Right now I didn't feel as though we were on speaking terms. I grabbed one of the lanterns lined up on shore and slogged my soggy sneakers down the path toward my cot. Maybe a quick shower and change of clothes before dinner would help lift my spirits. Or not.

I stood in the shower frantically turning knobs every which way I could think of. No water. Not a trickle. Not one drop. Cherie took the lantern and went off in search of our guide. Wearing even less than the gentleman in the original travel brochure, I peered up from the roofless stall into the pitch-black night. I thought of the wide variety of snakes and nocturnal predators that inhabited the area, all endowed with perfect night vision. I knew they were looking down at me with the same longing that I feel when I spot an ice-cream truck. My prayer life was instantly revitalized.

When Cherie returned, she explained that the water pipes weren't connected yet—and wouldn't be for another six weeks. At least that explained why the toilets wouldn't flush. I redressed and made my way to dinner. What a surprise. Fried piranha. Heads and all. Just looking at my plate made me long for monkey leftovers. Bedtime could not come soon enough.

Of course, if tomorrow my only food would be what I could catch, this toothy fish could be it for quite a while. I recalled the mammoth snail shell I'd seen earlier in the day. Maybe I could sneak along the saltshaker from the dinner table. Certainly I was fast enough to track a snail the size of a Chihuahua. A little sprinkle, a long stick, a little spark, and voilà! Escargot à la Amazon.

I toyed with my piranha then headed for bed. As I crawled between the sheets that who-knows-what had slept in last and pulled the mosquito netting over me like a shroud, the wildlife in the jungle sounded as though it were cranking up for an all-nighter. The humid night air felt so thick I could hardly breathe. Choking back tears didn't help. This time they flowed from fear, not awe.

I can't do this, God! I know I got myself into this mess, but I don't want to be here. I don't want to venture into the jungle alone. I don't want to hunt or fish or even walk around in squishy, stinky sneakers. I'm an outdoor wimp. I'll admit it. I know this isn't life or death—well, at least I hope not—but I'm so afraid of letting Cherie down and of making a complete fool of myself by pushing myself to do things I just can't do. You created me! You know my limits. Help . . .

"Vicki! Vicki!" Cherie's persistent whisper woke me from a sound sleep. "It's raining! Look!" A waterfall of rainwater was cascading off the tin roof into pond-sized puddles of mud on the ground below.

Thank You, God! We can't trek off into the jungle in a deluge, right? I turned over on my bed only to see Llaco's sleeping face on the cot next to me.

"I thought this was the 'girls' tent,'" I whispered to Cherie. Our guide's eyelids rolled up like venetian blinds.

"Oh no! It's raining!" Llaco cried, bouncing out of bed with the kind of energy I usually reserve for sometime later in the day. "I'm so sorry," he said with a profound sense of sadness. " I know how much this day meant to you all."

"That's OK," we replied, with the sincerest smiles we could muster.

"Maybe we'll just go fishing!" Llaco said, bounding through the wall of water that poured down the stairs.

Cherie and I gave each other the "he can't be serious" look. It was something we'd do a lot during the coming week. But the good news was that today God not only provided an escape from the dreaded "survivor" ordeal, but a complimentary shower! We grabbed our washcloths and headed outside.

We did go fishing that day. And the next. And the next . . . Well, you get the idea. We also hunted crocodile for soup. We saw glowworms light up lily pads at night like an enchanted fairy village. We watched pink dolphins jump from the river into the air at Llaco's call. We learned how to get fresh water and make face paint from jungle foliage.

We ate a lot, and I mean a lot, of piranha. I not only learned to like it but how to use my butter knife to saw out the teeth as souvenirs for friends.

On our final day together, Llaco presented me with a handmade "Piranha Queen" crown for catching more fish than anyone— including the master fisherman, who by the third day chose to leave his fancy tackle behind and imitate my "stick with string" technique. I was covered in mosquito bites; my ankles were swollen from fire-ant stings; I'd had a tarantula walk up my arm and survived (both me and the spider); my clothes smelled like dead fish; and my tennis shoes never dried. It had been quite a week.

From my cushioned seat at the back of the speedboat returning us to civilization, I watched the lopsided dugout canoe until it disappeared from my view. Tears filled my eyes yet again. They weren't because I was overwhelmed with relief to be going home (although I can't say I had a burning desire to stay). It was because at that moment I realized why God doesn't let me know the full itinerary for my life. If He did, I might hightail it and run the other direction, afraid I couldn't handle what's ahead.

My adversary, the Amazon, had proved to me that I was both weaker, and stronger, than I'd ever realized. I'd done what I never dreamed I'd do. Seen life I never imagined existed. And turned to God more frequently throughout the day than I had in years. If I'd known everything I'd have to face before I left on this trip, I never would have come—and I would have missed out on so much.

I turned forward in my seat, scanning the path of the river before me. Only God really knew what lay ahead. And that was just fine with me.

> *I can do everything with the help of Christ who*
> *gives me the strength I need.*
> Philippians 4:13 (NLT)

PERSONAL JOURNEY

HAVE you had a "detour" in your life where you ended up somewhere you never wanted to be, faced with doing something you never wanted to do? How did you and God relate throughout your experience? How did what happened change you?

WHAT does knowing you can do everything with Christ's help mean to you? Is there anything that makes Philippians 4:13 hard for you to believe? What do you think God does, and doesn't, mean in this verse?

WHAT does being "strong in the Lord" look like? Can you use these words to describe yourself? Why or why not?

READ 2 Corinthians 12:9–10. How are these words true in light of the story you've just read? In light of your own experiences?

LEARNING to catch piranha or deal with fire ants are minor tussles when compared with many of the struggles we'll face. But how can learning to rely on God's strength for little things help prepare us for times of real challenge?

Journey Toward . . .
HUMILITY

Beijing,
China

The message of the Chinese pastor's sermon, as translated through the whispers of a friend, struck straight to the heart.

She was four, maybe five. Dressed gaily in pink, she stood by her father's side in silence, her eyes wide and attentive. Two other men stood nearby on the potholed stone street. They, too, were silent, watching, waiting for the inevitable. The father pushed the lamb to the ground, put his foot on its neck, and raised the knife. I turned my head. That did nothing to block out the animal's final garbled cries.

I glanced back. The father, knife in hand, looked at me and smiled. The men laughed. I lowered my eyes, not wanting to look at the blood seeping into the drain below the animal's neck. Not wanting to reveal more of how timid I was in the face of a necessary sacrifice. Did I think the lamb I'd eaten for dinner had died in its sleep?

The image of the lamb, the knife, the blood, and the innocent eyes of a little girl in pink replayed in my mind as I raised the Communion bread to my lips. Since I was in a liturgical-style church, I knew I was supposed to voice some response, but the only Mandarin I knew was "hello," "thank you," "don't want" (useful with overzealous vendors), and "elephant" (useful absolutely nowhere except the zoo). I simply smiled, closed my eyes, and talked to the One who understood every word I said, no matter what language I was speaking.

In some ways I was as out of my element here in a Chinese church as I was on the streets of Chuandixia, the rustic mountain village where I'd seen the lamb slaughtered a few days before. Of course, for me, blending in anywhere in China was really not an option. At the breakfast buffet, I bypassed the fried chicken feet and balked at the dish labeled *braised ox appendage*. I occasionally flipped food onto the floor with my chopsticks. I was illiterate—couldn't read, couldn't write, couldn't even sound out words from the indecipherable Chinese characters. But even if I never opened my mouth or sat down for a meal, all it took was a glance to know I wasn't a local. The fair hair on my head stuck out like a kernel of corn amid a sea of black beans.

And it wasn't only with the Chinese that I didn't blend in. I was also an anomaly among the group with whom I was traveling. A spouse accompanying her husband on a business trip is always a bit like an unnecessary appendage. Perhaps my true peer group was the braised ox at the buffet.

It's not that my husband's business associates were inhospitable. They were all kind, congenial, quick to include me in their conversations. It was just that they all seemed so incredibly smart and well dressed. So business savvy. So professional. They were movers and shakers. As for me, I simply shook when I moved, thanks to the numerous dishes served at every Chinese meal.

Maybe I was more "Chinese" than I wanted to admit—overly concerned with "saving face." In a newspaper article, I'd read that the most common ways people in China tried to show a better "face" to others was by becoming adept at things others couldn't do; working to gain people's praise; becoming more knowledgeable than their peers; marrying a "better" spouse; holding an important title or position; or wearing brand-name clothing. It also noted that 87 percent of those polled felt saving face consumed too much of their time and energy. Make that 87 percent, plus one fairhaired tourist.

OK, God, what's up with me? I prayed as I received a small plastic cup of juice made from the pulp of some unidentifiable fruit. *Nothing new. . . .* I felt in response. *Just the same battle I fight every day. Who do I choose to serve? God or myself? Am I more concerned about saving my own face or allowing God's image to shine through me? When I travel and try to adapt to the culture and learn a bit of the language, am I doing it out of respect for the people I'm interacting with or trying to save face by attempting to blend in?*

The message of the Chinese pastor's sermon, as translated through the whispers of a friend, struck straight to the heart. As always, God's words and timing were perfect. As I caught bits and pieces of the sermon, God's Spirit wove the pastor's words in with my own thoughts to tell a story of betrayal and redemption. Judas's story. Peter's story. My story . . .

Judas walked with Jesus. Talked with Him. Even called Him friend. But after spending three years with the Messiah, Judas still didn't fully accept who He was. Judas betrayed Jesus for 30 pieces of silver, for a mere 30 kwai. Then, unable to reconcile repentance with losing face, Judas hung himself.

Peter betrayed Jesus that same night. But Peter's shame over what he'd done led him toward reconciliation instead of despair. By humbly losing face, Peter saved something more valuable—his soul. Every time I put my own face before God's, every time I choose to spend my time, energy, resources, and love on my ways, instead of His, I sell Jesus for 30 kwai. The only question that remained was whose example would I follow? Judas's or Peter's?

That evening, in the company of strangers, I chose (as I'd done so many times in the past) to lose face and confess, to choose humility over pride. To let God's forgiveness flow over me. To dance to the rhythms of grace. To begin again, washed as white as snow by a Lamb slain for me.

As the church service ended, I walked outside into the cool night air. Refreshed. Renewed. Not only wholly loved, but feeling truly whole. I felt at home in the crush of God's children. We'd filled the church building and two side rooms, overflowed into classrooms, then into the front courtyard and the alley right into the street. That night I'd joined more than 1,000 people in making a choice to save face or lose it for Christ. It was the fourth service of the day at one of the few government-sanctioned churches in Beijing; yet I knew even more of God's children had come together this Sunday throughout the city, and beyond. Some of them met freely, while others worshipped in secret. Some prayed like Paul, from the confines of a prison cell. But God was with His children in China, in America, around the world—wherever they happened to be tonight.

Tomorrow I'd pack my dirty clothes, enjoy my last buffet, and head back to the place where I could blend in—if I wanted to. I hadn't bought myself a souvenir on this trip, but God had tattooed a Chinese character on my heart. The character for "righteousness." It's formed by placing the character for "lamb" above the character for "me." The Lamb of God covering me is the only way that allows my flawed self to walk in righteousness.

God's goal isn't to help me blend in, but to stand out. To be light in darkness. Truth amid lies. Salt in a tasteless society. A child, standing by her Father's side, wide-eyed and attentive, willing to lose face to save her soul.

> *"Look, the Lamb of God, who takes away the sins of the world!"*
> John 1:29 (NIV)

PERSONAL JOURNEY

ARE there any ways you try and blend in with those around you? At work? At school? At church? With friends? With family? Why?

HUMILITY is not thinking you're worth less than you are, but seeing yourself the same way God does. Read James 4:10. How can people humble themselves?

IF God already knows everything you've done, why do you think He tells you to confess your sins to Him? (See 1 John 1:8–9.)

IS there any area in your life where you're selling Jesus for 30 kwai? If so, take some time alone with God and put 1 John 1:8–9 into practice.

FOR some of the same reasons I didn't want to watch a lamb being killed, we often shy away from taking a good look at the reality of Jesus' sacrifice. Why is it important not to gloss over what happened? Read Revelation 5:12. Then picture yourself with all of God's children from around the world and throughout time singing these words. Thank God for what He's done!

Machu Picchu,

Peru

Rain was coming at me from every which way but up. Mud happened to have the corner on that direction. The combination of the two slowed my steps down to a slip-sliding shuffle. Morning had been a cloudless, sticky swelter, so I'd donned shorts. Now, a steady waterfall of raindrops cascaded off my rain jacket, down over my bare knees, and onto my hiking boots. No longer brand spanking new, my boots

There hung a single cloud on an otherwise crystal-clear, cloudless night. But I'd never seen a cloud move like this before.

were also no longer purple, but soppy sludge brown.

I consoled myself with the thought that there wasn't a mirror anywhere within a good ten miles. Even with a hood, my hair was as wet and flat as a proverbial Peruvian pancake. Unfortunately, I couldn't make the same claim for the trail. It was wet, all right, but certainly not flat. At times it felt like the only direction the Inca Trail went was straight up toward the clouds. Now we were smack-dab in the middle of them. How far up could we go from here?

A porter, his feet and sandals caked in gritty goo, flew by me at a vigorous sprint. Another followed close at his heels. "They're afraid of ghosts," our guide, Manolo, explained. "This cloud forest is full of stories." So was Manolo.

The one I couldn't get out of my mind was his "true-life" tale supposedly told by those who camped just over Dead Woman's Pass in the Valley of the Ghosts. Personally, I figured if the topography had been named Laughing Ladies' Summit and the Valley of the Bonbons, the campers' imaginations probably wouldn't have gotten so out of hand. But I digress.

As the story goes, campers awakened in the middle of the night to find a young girl in Incan attire standing in their tent. Having heard rumors that children were murdered on this grassy plain between Warmiwanusca and the next mountain pass—either by hostile Spanish conquistadors or as a ritual sacrifice by Incan rulers—the campers figured they were nose-to-nose with a ghost. So they did the only thing they could think of. One of them tossed their left shoe. The girl disappeared.

Supposedly this phantom materialized on several occasions to different groups of campers, which is why most hikers now camp on the opposite side of the pass. And why I'd noticed our porters racing through that valley wearing a terror-stricken look on their faces earlier in the day. They wore that same look now. Only this time raindrops ran off their faces too.

I'd read that over 250 species of orchids, rare birds, and animals in danger of extinction thrived in the junglelike growth that surrounded me. But at the moment all I could see was brush and mud blurred through a veil of rainy mist—and the only thing in danger of extinction was my enthusiasm.

"We're almost there," Manolo said, trying to bolster our soggy spirits. "Only an hour more!"

"Up?" I asked.

Manolo simply smiled. We plodded on.

When our waterlogged group of hikers finally slogged into camp, the tents were already pitched and dinner was waiting to be served. Guess the threat of ghosts does have its upside. After changing into something a little less damp, I joined my fellow trekkers around the wobbly camp table for a feast of squash soup, stir-fried meat and potatoes, and steaming cups of coca tea (to fend off altitude sickness). Sheets of rain relentlessly pounded on the tented roof of our wind-whipped dining room. But inside, life was good. We were toasty warm, reasonably dry, and didn't have to walk further than 50 feet until after sunrise. Bad jokes, tall tales, pistachio nuts, and a flask of something that smelled as if it could disinfect the inside of my hiking boots were passed around the table. I passed on all but the nuts and tall tales.

But my mind kept drifting toward the final stretch of our journey. Only five or six more hours of hiking and I'd step into the pages of the book I'd explored as a child. I'd be standing, at last, where the Incas had stood, face-to-face with the mystery that had carved out a sacred place in my soul. The little girl inside couldn't stay seated any longer. Like Christmas Eve, the earlier I went to sleep, the earlier the "big day" would come. I opened the tent flap to head to bed.

As soon as I stepped outside, I froze. Words fled like frightened field mice. The rain had stopped. The clouds had cleared. In their place was a wall of white so bright my mind could hardly accept the fact that what I was looking at was real. I'd only witnessed majesty like this in my dreams. My knees nearly gave way in unbridled awe.

Like a featured performer standing against the velvet curtain of night, the snow-covered peak appeared to be lit by a spotlight. But this was only the reflection of a not quite full moon. The horizon before me was almost filled edge to edge by the glowing summit. The scene looked close enough to touch, as though God had placed a flat backdrop behind my tent, a photograph of a mountain blown up to five times its normal size. So blindingly surreal, yet so invitingly breathtaking, I instinctively reached out my hand in wonder.

"Mount Salcantay," Manolo commented as he passed me on the way to his tent. "It means, 'the one who cannot be tamed.'"

I could understand why. At almost 20,600 feet, it made the "14ers" I'd admired in Colorado look like gopher mounds. Wave after wave of praise flowed through me. No words. No sound. Just gratitude, awe, and wellsprings of joy. Like Moses, I, too, stood on hallowed ground. And I felt as though the Almighty had just passed by.

When I finally managed to tear my eyes away from the mountain and enter my tent, I knew my night's sleep would be peaceful. Salcantay, my watchtower, would stand guard through the night.

Morning broke clear and crisp with a hint of mist still sleeping in the valley below. I brushed the dried mud off my purple hiking boots as Salcantay looked on. Yesterday was behind me. Machu Picchu lay ahead.

I'd like to say that my feet fairly flew over the trail those last six hours. But they remained earthbound, plodding along one step at a time, and true to form, usually bringing up the rear. But that was OK by me. My heart was light, even if my daypack was not. Although the trail still had its fair share of "up," for once there was ample "down." Hundreds of white stone steps wound their way over rocky cliffs, twisting around trees and between boulders—an Incan Stairmaster on the narrow ledge of a sheer rock face.

When I found myself facing the final flight of stairs, knowing my first glimpse of Machu Picchu was right over the rise, I had a sudden impulse to turn and run. To head back the direction I'd just come from. That path was known, familiar, safe. I wanted to return to the comfort of Salcantay, to zip myself up in my tent and take a lifelong nap. I felt unprepared. Queasy. Teetering on the edge of embarrassment. And this time I couldn't blame it on altitude sickness.

You are now certifiably crazy! I scolded myself. *You come all this way, push yourself beyond what any rational person in your pathetic condition would do, and now you want to turn back? You don't deserve to be here! Why should you have the privilege of fulfilling a dream—and a silly one at that? You're a failure. A fraud. And you'll never change!*

All the insecurities I thought had died on Dead Woman's Pass arose like Lazarus from the grave. Sure, I'd won a strategic battle on the slope of Warmiwanusca, but the war raged on. My emotions battled reason. My insecurities battled truth. My God battled and conquered an enemy that often felt more like a figment of my imagination than an actual adversary. On the cusp of fulfilling a childhood dream, my life felt as filled with mountains and valleys as the Inca Trail itself. But I knew there was so much more going on than what could be seen with my eyes.

My entrance into Machu Picchu marked the fulfillment of a dream, but also the end of a much-anticipated journey. Reality waited on the other side of Intipunku, "the Sun Gate" into the Incan ruins that stood as a sentinel at the top of these stairs. What if Machu Picchu didn't live up to 30 years of expectation? What if I'd walked all this way for nothing? Then again, what if this really would be a dream come true? In 24 hours after saying hello to my dream, I'd be saying good-bye.

Delight yourself in Me and I'll give you the desires of your heart. . . . God's reassuring words quelled the other noisy dialogue waging war in my brain. I took one long deep breath, gathered what few wits I had left about me, and did what I'd done for the last four days. I put one foot in front of the other and headed up toward the clouds.

As I crested the final set of the steps, the library book I'd lost myself in as a kid opened its pages to me, this time in 3-D. I stepped in. Reality was even better than fantasy. The little girl within kicked up her heels wanting to skip, giggle, and play "hide-and-seek" among the ruins. I contained her. Barely.

The setting was wilder, steeper, greener, than any photo could ever capture. Snow-frosted peaks towered over the ruins from every direction. Over 100 stone structures sprawled over the uneven terrain, a mosaic of white granite edged in emerald. Terraces spilled down the sides of the cliffs, along with a single winding road that led to the valley floor. And the tourists, well, they were everywhere. Somehow they'd never made it into my dreams. But they certainly had made it here today.

Our guide assured us that by 4:00 P.M. they'd be gone. Tightly packed into buses, they'd travel down that one road and catch the train back to Cuzco, their day trip complete. But not us. We were more than mere tourists. We were explorers, sojourners, pilgrims who had suffered to reach our goal. And we were here through the night until late the next day. I could feel our group's cumulative pride puff up.

Sure, those day-trippers had experienced a taste of Machu Picchu's mystery, but I wanted to immerse myself in it. Not waste a minute! Well, after I immersed myself in the hotel's bathtub, scrubbed off a couple layers of grime, shaved the protective layer of fur from my legs, and had something cold to drink. Something with real ice cubes in it. One can only take that whole "adventurer" thing so far.

But to take full advantage of the time we had, my friend Cherie and I made a pact: tonight we'd explore Machu Picchu by moonlight.

That evening, five bucks to the guard at the gatehouse gained us entrance. Everything was going according to plan—except I never planned on everything being so creepy. What looked inviting by day was foreboding by night. Shadows cast by the megawatt moon transformed stone niches into hollow eyes that seemed to follow my every move. The precipices that bordered three sides of the site became craggy bottomless pits. Llamas wandered the ruins like specters, appearing and disappearing between the granite walls. The ruins themselves glowed a ghostly gray. My dream come true began to feel more like a nightmare.

I tried to shrug it off, this feeling of being watched, though no one else wandered the grounds but Cherie, some llamas, and me. But when Cherie spoke it was in a whisper, as though to prevent someone from overhearing what was said. It wasn't just me. There was something more here than met the eye.

Cherie and I carefully picked our way through the shadows to the sacristy, the highest central point of the ruins. Our rubber-soled hiking boots made a soft tapping sound on the stone steps, which echoed like gunshots in the deathly still night. At the top, we surveyed our surroundings.

No one can say with real certainty what happened here. What this site was used for. Why it was abandoned almost 500 years ago. Why almost 90 percent of the more than 100 skeletal remains uncovered here have been female. At one time, archaeologists believed Machu Picchu was a city populated by women specially chosen to cater to the needs of Incan rulers. Today all that's generally agreed upon, because of the abundance of ornamental stonework, is that this was an important ceremonial site.

The carved pillar before us supported that claim. Six feet tall and cut from one solid piece of granite bedrock, it resembled a sundial rising from a stone table. But Intihuatana, the "Hitching Post of the Sun," was used to chart the time of year and predict the summer and winter solstice. In designing a "hitching post," Incan sculptors cut away any portion of stone they felt did not possess a holy quality, referred to as *huaca*. The Spanish conquistadors crushed every Intihuatana they found, trying to eradicate the Inca's worship of the sun. The one that stood before me was the tallest of its kind still in existence.

Maybe that's why this place felt so ominous and eerie. I'd never been one to feel spiritually uneasy around ancient ritual sites, but this one was different. After all, I'd given it a sacred place in my heart.

"Do you see that?" Cherie said in a hoarse whisper. She was staring at the edge of the cliff right below us. There hung a single cloud on an otherwise crystal-clear, cloudless night. But I'd never seen a cloud move like this before. Instead of floating up in the sky—where clouds belong—this one crept up over the edge of the cliff, then clung to the ground like a snake slowly winding its way in our direction.

"Should I toss my left hiking boot?" Cherie asked. I froze like I had before Salcantay, only this time in fear, instead of awe.

A whispered plea flowed out of my mouth like a breath. "Jesus, . . ."

In an instant, the cloud seemed to scatter in every direction. Then it was gone. And so were we.

On our way back to the hotel, Cherie and I tried to act nonchalant. Unsure of what we'd seen, unsure of what to say, trying to convince ourselves that we were simply two overtired travelers with overactive imaginations. But that night my dreams made me cry out in the dark.

The next day, Machu Picchu returned to its fairy-tale image in my eyes. But in my heart, something had shifted. I wandered slowly through the ruins toward a seldom-visited site, this time alone. Far from the crowds that were already starting to lean against ancient stone walls and pose for photos on Intihuatana, I sat on a rock to talk with God.

Questions. I always had questions. And sometimes, many times, there were no answers. I wasn't sure of what to make of the night before. Natural phenomenon? Creative mind gone wild? A spiritual manifestation of my emotional roller coaster? Who knew? What I did know was that Machu Picchu was nothing more than a place. A place where people had been drawn to mystery, just like me. They looked to the sun because they didn't know where else to turn. I did.

I turned to the One who made the sun and set it on its course in the sky. To the One full of mystery, as well as majesty. To the One who reminded me there was more to life than I could see with my eyes; that I had an enemy, as well as an Almighty in my life. I turned to God, my Salcantay—the One who cannot be tamed.

> *More and more people are seeing this: they enter*
> *the mystery, abandoning themselves to God.*
> Psalm 40:3 (*The Message*)

PERSONAL JOURNEY

IN James 1:5, God says that if you need wisdom, all you need to do is ask for it. Why isn't wisdom enough to answer all our questions and solve all the "mysteries" of God's world? What light does Isaiah 55:8–9 shed on this?

DO you believe there's a literal enemy, as well as an Almighty? If so, what do you think this enemy is like? List any Scriptures you can find to back this up.

THROUGHOUT the Scriptures, the enemy is called by many different names: accuser, tempter, deceiver, slanderer, the devil, and Satan. The name Satan literally means "adversary." How can you see the "adversary" at work in this chapter? How have you seen him at work in your life?

READ James 4:7. Why is our adversary nothing to fear? What practical steps can you take to send him to turn on his heels and run?

HOW does remembering there's more to this life than what you can see with your eyes change how you view your current problems? Your victories? Your future?

Florence,

Italy

W e were newlyweds on a hike. What could be more romantic? My husband and I were following an overgrown forest path to a spot I'd happened upon a few years before. I warmly recalled walking that same trail by myself one afternoon and discovering a rustic A-frame cabin. Today I was excited to share my secret place with the one I wanted to share all my secrets with.

I wondered what perspective the personal tour group I was herding through Florence's crowded streets had about what they saw.

When we came around the final bend, my feet came to a confused halt. I was underwhelmed, not to mention embarrassed. The A-frame I'd constructed in my mind was really a ramshackle wooden lean-to barely larger than an orange crate. That one little "miscalculation" has become family legend. My daughter, Katrina, summed it up best one day when she said, "If you want the real story, you'll find it somewhere between Mom and Dad. Mom exaggerates. Dad minimizes."

Now I want to assure you, I don't exaggerate. I say things exactly as they are—or should I say, exactly as I perceive them to be. Which is why I was so nervous about taking my husband to Florence, Italy. It had been almost 30 years since I'd lived there and I was really looking forward to a stroll down memory lane. But as a woman teetering on the brink of menopause, what if I couldn't even remember where memory lane was?

After all, on our newlywed hike, my brain was still fresh and youthful. When I hit my mid-40s I felt as if someone took all my nicely organized mental file folders and dropped them on the floor, leaving me scrambling for the right word. Lately, just recalling my kids' names was a challenge. (OK, so that is an exaggeration.) But what if Florence didn't live up to my own mental hype? What if Michelangelo's *David* wasn't the perfectly sculpted marble giant I recalled? What if David was really the size of a dashboard bobble-head?

To add to the pressure, four other friends would be joining us, one of them being my father-in-law. All of these dear people were looking to me, the "local," to act as tour guide, menu translator, and human GPS. As our departure date grew closer, my long anticipated trip "home" began to feel more like a college entrance exam.

But as the landing gear of the plane touched down at the Amerigo Vespucci Airport in Florence, all I felt was excitement. I was home: Even though I'd only lived here for ten months, Florence was my first taste of adult freedom. And what a taste it was . . . renting my first apartment, taking a train to anywhere and everywhere on the weekends, learning a new language, and trying to grow in my newfound faith in a city where I couldn't even find an English-speaking church. I couldn't wait to drop off our luggage and hit the streets.

One benefit of returning to a city that is a UNESCO world heritage site is that chances are pretty good you won't find your favorite landmark torn down to make way for a minimart. Even after 28 years, I found so many things were exactly the way I left them. The Ponte Vecchio, the Duomo, the Boboli Gardens, and yes, even the *David*.

But squeezing the history, art, and architecture of Florence into a visit of only seven days can be overwhelming. Some people actually become dizzy, lose consciousness, and wind up in the hospital due to the overload of beauty in this Renaissance city. (No, I'm not making this up!) It's called Stendhal's syndrome and about 12 cases are documented in Florence each year.

Of course, two people can look at the same thing and come away feeling totally different, weak-kneed and woozy, awed and appreciative, or perhaps even emotionally unmoved. It all depends on how individuals perceive what they are seeing. It depends on their perspective.

I wondered what perspective the personal tour group I was herding through Florence's crowded streets had about what they saw. They were so open, genial, and willing to follow wherever I led that I began to get nervous all over again. Every "So, what would you like to see today?" was met with "I don't care. . . . You choose. . . . Anywhere you take us is fine." But what if my favorite places weren't theirs? What if they didn't perceive beauty the same way I did?

For the first few days, I felt fairly confident. We hit all the top tourist attractions, along with the other ten kajillion foreign visitors who happened to be in town. Three decades had sure made a difference there. As a student, I remember having the Church of San Lorenzo completely to myself. I'd often stop by after school, simply to bask in the contrast of the ornate grandiosity of Medici's tomb with the clean, simple lines of Michelangelo's sculptures of *Dawn* and *Dusk*. No longer. Now I not only had to share my "personal" treasure with the crush of perpetual crowds, but I actually had to pay to get in—only to find much of the chapel obscured by a modern web of renovation scaffolding.

But there was one place I wanted to take my convivial little group that wasn't always found on the typical whirlwind tour map: the Church of Santa Maria del Carmine. My chance came near the end of our trip. We started out early, heading away from the snarled streets of downtown into the quiet neighborhoods of Santo Spirito.

We passed single-room grocers, shimmying our way around pyramids of produce proudly displayed on the single-file sidewalk. I bid *"Buon giorno"* to one of my favorite fountains, a bearded old man spewing water from his gaily pursued lips. Neighborhood gossip drifted out onto the street, along with the scent of freshly baked bread from the numerous small bakeries along the way. Parents called out words of affection, and last-minute instructions, from windows and doorways in the direction of children heading off to school. Block after block, we walked in the shadow of green-shuttered buildings, now family apartments, yet almost all of them centuries old. Here, the past 30 years fell away. This felt more like the Florence I knew. This felt like "home."

But time hadn't totally stood still. We did have to pay to visit the Brancacci Chapel inside the church. And as they say in Italy, the tickets were *molto caro* (very dear). But for me it was money well spent.

For over 500 years, the frescoes of the Brancacci Chapel have told the story of the life of Peter, bookended by Adam and Eve's expulsion from the Garden of Eden. When the Church of Santa Maria del Carmine almost burned to the ground in 1771, the Brancacci Chapel remained untouched by the flames—for which I couldn't help but offer a personal prayer of thanks.

I stood in the small open-ended chapel, drinking in the vibrant colors of the visual narration. The frescoes were an interesting contrast of styles, since they were painted by three separate men: Masolino, who was commissioned to do the work for a wealthy merchant named Brancacci; Masaccio, Masolino's apprentice; and Filippino Lippi, who finished the chapel 50 years after it was begun.

Though Masolino was the master, it's Masaccio whose work is most celebrated. That's because Masaccio accomplished something on these walls that had never been achieved in painting before. He incorporated linear perspective. Perspective had been seen in both architecture and sculpture before this point, but it had never been captured on flat canvas. At the time, this was such a fresh approach to "seeing" a scene that both Michelangelo and Leonardo da Vinci came to stand where I stood now, to study and to learn. Masaccio's work in the Brancacci Chapel was so revolutionary that it was considered to be the first truly Renaissance painting.

I remembered learning how to draw a box in perspective sometime during junior high. You draw one square, then another square overlapping it a bit to the left or right. You join the corners with straight lines and voilà! You have a box that looks dimensional, instead of flat. My notebooks were covered with countless box doodles. Little did I know then that I was a student of Masaccio.

Perspective invited me into the stories on the walls of the chapel. I wasn't just an observer. I was part of the crowd, witnessing Peter healing the sick or pulling a coin from the mouth of a fish to pay taxes. But perspective didn't stop there. It reminded me there was a vanishing point, a horizon that faded from view. What was closest to me was larger, more immediately grabbing my attention. What was in the distance was undersized, as is everything that's distorted by the perspective of the human eye. The distant scenery whispered, "Remember, the landscape is larger than what you can see."

But Masaccio's talent extended beyond linear perspective. It was the emotion depicted on the faces of the people he'd painted that tugged at my heart. The frescoes around the chapel both began, and ended, with Adam and Eve being driven out of the Garden of Eden. One scene was by Masolino, the other Masaccio. Masolino's Adam and Eve looked like they were posing for a formal family portrait. They seemed as nonplussed as a couple who've just been informed by the flight attendant that their seats have been changed from row 14 to 20.

In contrast, Masaccio's Adam and Eve are in agony. They've just suffered a shocking change of perspective. One act of disobedience has moved them from "I'm loved" to "I'm naked." Adam hangs his head in shame. His shoulders sag with the weight of the consequences he's suffering. His hands cover his face, hiding his tears from view. Eve's face is turned upward, as if lamenting aloud, "What have I done?" Her features are contorted with tears, her hands attempting to disguise the nakedness she now feels.

I'd felt it too . . . the nakedness, the shame, the guilt. In Masaccio's Eve, I saw a picture of myself. And like Eve, my perspective had undergone a nearly inconceivable change. The difference was, I'd been welcomed back into the garden. The head that once hung in shame is now raised. My eyes are lifted to the skies as a chorus of thanksgiving flows from deep within my heart. I stand naked, wholly exposed before God. But I'm no longer ashamed. His forgiveness has clothed me in grace.

I see life differently now. My perspective began to shift the day I chose to acknowledge that God is God—and I am not. I'm no longer only an observer, going through the motions of life. God has painted the details, the beauty, and the purpose of every journey, both past and present, with deeper hues of significance. Now I can see that I'm part of the story, His story. A story extends far beyond this world right into the next. And that's no exaggeration.

> *Pursue the things over which Christ presides.*
> *Don't shuffle along, eyes to the ground, absorbed*
> *with the things right in front of you. Look up,*
> *and be alert to what is going on around Christ—*
> *that's where the action is. See things from his*
> *perspective.*
> Colossians 3:1–2 (*The Message*)

PERSONAL JOURNEY

FIRST Peter 1:18 (*The Message*) says, "Your life is a journey you must travel with a deep consciousness of God." How has this God-consciousness changed your perspective on life and your role in it?

IN this chapter I mentioned how our perception plays an important role in our perspective. If someone perceives that either God is a myth or simply uninvolved in this world, what might his or her perspective of life be like? How can you help this person better understand God's perspective?

WHAT are some practical ways you can better understand someone else's perspective, thereby better understanding the heart of that individual?

ARE you currently facing a situation in which you need a better grasp of God's perspective? Take time right now to pray about this. James 1:5 assures you that God will provide the wisdom you need.

MASACCIO may be the most famous Renaissance painter people have never heard of. That's because he died at 27, only one year after his work on the Brancacci Chapel. No matter how young or old you are, you have a vital place in God's story. Ask God to help you better understand the unique role you have.

Journey Toward . . .
HOME

From Phoenix to Heaven

N o matter how amazing a journey is—how incredible the sights I've seen, how precious the new friends I've made, or how deeply my heart has been changed in the process—there's always something that pulls me back, a tether that tugs me in the direction of home. Home to what's safe and familiar. Home to those I know and love. Home . . . where I am known.

I love the severity of the desert landscape, the power of the summer monsoon, and the fact that I hardly ever have to wear socks.

Currently, Phoenix, Arizona, holds that title. But having been a desert dweller for only 2 years, I don't consider myself a full-fledged Phoenician. (Which for someone enamored with ancient cultures seems intrinsically wrong to begin with.) However, you'd assume that since I love to travel, making a move to a new locale would be easy. You'd be wrong. Colorado Springs had been home for more than 20 years when my husband casually mentioned one evening over dinner, "So, what would you think of moving to Arizona?"

I answered candidly (as I have been known to do), "Certainly God would not move us from heaven to hell!" But that's exactly what God did.

Arizona isn't hell, even though the summer temperatures in Phoenix can instill a fire-and-brimstone sermon with a bit of a "been there, done that" feel. Actually, I've settled into Phoenix quite nicely. I like preparing for "winter" by nestling bedding plants in potting soil. I enjoy eating outside on the patio for months on end. I love the severity of the desert landscape, the power of the summer monsoon, and the fact that I hardly ever have to wear socks. As for the friends I've met? I can't picture my life without them.

So if tonight over dinner my husband were to ask me, "What would you think of moving to Timbuktu?" I'd probably throw a fit. No matter how great Timbuktu could turn out to be.

Would I do the same with God? If He told me He was changing my address to heaven, effective immediately, would I dig in my heels and cry, "No, I want life! Life!" Would I cling to the landscape I'm familiar with simply because *life* is the only home I've ever known?

The truth is that heaven is not *terra incognita* (unknown territory). God imprinted the coordinates for its location on my soul as indelibly as He did the pattern of my DNA on every cell of my body. Second Corinthians 5:5 (*The Message*) says that God "puts a little of heaven in our hearts so that we'll never settle for less." I've felt that piece of heaven. It's the source of my wanderlust, pulling me toward God and His throne like a built-in homing device.

Each time I'm drawn to explore an unfamiliar shore, or drawn back home again, what I'm really searching for is paradise, the kind of heavenly home I was created to inhabit. That's why even in the face of adventure, wonder, and beauty, there's still a hint of discontent. It's not because I've been jaded by my travels. It's because that God-given piece of heaven whispers that there's so much more I was made for; this is just a tiny taste of what's to come. That's why even though I love this earth and the life God has so graciously given me, the journey I anticipate most is the one that will lead me Home . . . where I am truly known.

A new heaven and earth awaits us all. And this present world with all its breathtaking wonders that at one time so easily capture our imaginations, beckoning us toward journeys of God-inspired discovery, will be replaced by a paradise for which mere words will be too commonplace to fully describe. The God we catch only glimpses of while we are here on earth will stand before us in glory. Our knees will buckle in worship. Our tongues will cry out the truest words ever sung, as we bask in the full presence of Holy, Holy, Holy. Tears and good-byes will be a thing of the past. Our joyous new journey, one without end, will have finally begun.

> *How blessed all those in whom you live, whose lives become roads you travel; they wind through lonesome valleys, come upon brooks, discover cool springs and pools brimming with rain! God-traveled, these roads curve up the mountain, and at the last turn—Zion! God in full view!*
> Psalm 84:5–7 (*The Message*)

PERSONAL JOURNEY

HOW have the 30 journeys you've taken in this book changed your view of the world? Of travel? Of God? Of yourself?

HEBREWS 13:14 (NLT) tells us "this world is not our home." What is it then? What is your place in the world—and its place in you?

ARE you familiar with that piece of heaven that 2 Corinthians 5:5 says God has placed in your heart? How have you experienced a spiritual tug toward your home in heaven?

READ John 14:1–7. Mull over Jesus's words. If He knows you better than anyone else ever has, what kind of place do you think He would prepare especially for you?

RETREAT to a quiet place. Spend some time talking to God about the day you'll fully enter His presence, the day you'll meet Him face-to-face. Let your expectations, anticipation, and even your fears travel straight from your heart to heaven's throne.

New Hope® Publishers is a division of WMU®, an international organization that challenges Christian believers to understand and be radically involved in God's mission. For more information about WMU, go to www.wmu.com. More information about New Hope books may be found at www.newhopepublishers.com. New Hope books may be purchased at your local bookstore.

Other Books for Your Enjoyment

Born to Be Wild
Rediscover the Freedom of Fun
Jill Baughan
ISBN-10: 1-59669-048-8

Refresh
Sharing Stories. Building Faith.
Kathy Escobar and Laura Greiner
ISBN-13: 978-1-59669-069-1

5 Leadership Essentials for Women
*Developing Your Ability to Make Things
Happen*
Linda Clark
ISBN-10: 1-56309-842-3

Available in bookstores everywhere.

For information about these books or any New Hope product
visit www.newhopepublishers.com.